D1553812

DIVORCE
in the Parsonage

DIVORCE
in the Parsonage

Mary LaGrand Bouma

 Bethany Fellowship INC.
MINNEAPOLIS, MINNESOTA 55438

Published by Bethany Fellowship, Inc.
6820 Auto Club Road, Minneapolis, Minnesota 55438

Printed in the United States of America

Library of Congress Cataloging in Publication Data

Bouma, Mary LaGrand.
   Divorce in the parsonage.

   Bibliography: p.
   1. Clergy—Divorce. I. Title.
BV4395.5.B68   248'.892   79-16157
ISBN 0-87123-109-3

About the Author

MARY LA GRAND BOUMA is the wife of a Christian Reformed pastor and the mother of four children. She has a degree in French and English from Calvin College. Mrs. Bouma's articles have been published in *Christianity Today* as well as in national Christian Reformed publications. In 1969, she was selected regional *Homemaker of the Year* for *Family Circle* magazine. Her first book is *The Creative Homemaker*, Bethany Fellowship, 1973.

Contents

Introduction

During the last twenty-five years or so divorce has become increasingly more common in the United States and Canada. It has also gained social respectability. In fact, as a recent article in *Family Circle* put it, "A kind of moral backlash seems to have set in. Divorce isn't just being sanctioned now, it's virtually being sponsored. A profusion of books and articles is making the argument that lasting commitments aren't viable, that the risks involved in splitting up are manageable and that people's personal selves are likely to thrive on dissolution." [1]

Historically, the people of the United States have refused to accept divorced people as their political leaders. Until the middle of this century to divorce one's wife was to commit political suicide. Then the climate began to shift. Governor Nelson Rockefeller took a chance by divorcing his wife and got away with it. Soon other government officials did the same. By the time President Ford was under investigation for the vice-presidential nomination, his wife's previous divorce was not even a consideration in the inquiries. As a result, we now have a number of divorced governors, congressmen, senators, and other high government officials.

In the minds of many, the last defense against this growing social disorder was the clergy. Of course marriages among the clergy were invulnerable! But we found it was not so. Perhaps at first it was a rumor. A minister from another denomination was getting a divorce. He was an acquaintance of a distant relative. But then the rumors moved closer to home, within our own denomination. It was shocking, but soon forgotten. It must have been an isolated instance. Eventually, however, divorce began to separate our closest friends and former classmates. Cases such as this have multiplied many times, and today most of us can probably name half a dozen divorced ministers or ex-ministers. Lucille Lavender in her book *They Cry Too* says, "Among professionals, clergymen rank third in the number of divorces granted each year." [2]

Having been a pastor's wife for nineteen years, I know all too well the tremendous responsibilities and pressures that go along with the ministry. I know about the unfair expectations, about the pedestal position from which it is so easy to fall, and about the loneliness and sense of failure in the face of a job which is seemingly too big for anyone.

I also know, however, that God gives us the grace to handle whatever He calls us to do. When I think of the ministry I like to think of Ken Taylor's paraphrase of Philippians 4:13: "For I can do everything God asks me to with the help of Christ who gives me the strength and power." [3] Obviously there are rewards, privileges, and joys which are uniquely a part of the ministry. Although we have special problems, we also have special status. We're where the action is. We're not spectators, looking at what's happening out there. We're right in the middle for better or for worse, helping it happen.

Being a minister or a minister's wife is not for the fainthearted. I have interviewed scores of pastors and their wives across the country. They have various levels of formal education and come from differing backgrounds and social settings. But two things they have in common: vibrancy and commitment—both to Christ and to their work in his kingdom. Most, however, are experiencing some degree of frustration, and some are almost overwhelmed by difficulties. These people are not losers, though. They are trying diligently not only to cope with their problems, but also to rise above their circumstances. They have a lot of enthusiasm and a positive attitude—sometimes in the face of seemingly intolerable situations. It is their perseverence and trust in the Lord that is helping to change this world.

There is a darker side to the picture, however. A small minority of pastors and their wives are no longer finding it possible to cope. They are giving up the ministry, or their marriages, or both. And this group is growing at an alarming rate. This is not only a tremendous loss of talent and leadership for the Christian community; it is also a waste of personal fulfillment and an unnecessary devastation of families.

I believe that the tide can be turned. Foundering marriages among the clergy can be rescued. Disillusioned and disheartened pastors and wives can receive new direction and confidence. That is the message of this book.

My hope is that this book will be read by ministers, their wives, seminary students, those women planning to marry ministers, and perhaps most important of all, by church members to whom these flawed and sometimes bumbling—but nonetheless willing and dedicated—men and women of God are trying to minister.

The first chapter contains case histories, dramatic stories of failure in marriages among the clergy. These are not pretty stories, but they are true. I have tried to relate the facts as they were actually told to me, yet still preserving each person's anonymity. Obviously, these case histories do not represent the typical pastor, but neither are they isolated examples. I did not embroider them for dramatic effect, nor did I tone them down. The stark realities of this growing problem must be examined before a solution can be presented.

The next section is entitled the "Walking Wounded." Here I have tried to highlight the hurts and problems of everyday life inside the parsonage from the point of view of pastors, their wives, and their children. Perhaps most pastors and their wives will easily identify with this section.

Since I believe that these problems can be solved and that tragedy in pastoral marriages can be avoided, the last half of the book gives some very positive answers. Working out these solutions will involve the entire Christian community cooperating together. For this reason the book is written for all church members. There are separate chapters addressed to the specific problems of seminarians, their wives or girlfriends, pastors, pastors' wives, and congregations. There are also sections addressed to elders and deacons and to Christian psychologists who counsel pastors. However, while separate chapters may be read with profit, the book should be read in its entirety in order for its positive message to come through.

Acknowledgments

I'm sure no one writes a book without a lot of cooperation from others. This one required help from more people than I can name. First of all, there were the nearly 200 pastors, wives, ex-pastors, and ex-wives who so willingly met me in churches, motels, homes, and even a hospital in large cities and small towns from Seattle, Portland and San Francisco to Long Island, New York, and points in between. They came on their own time, with their own transportation, and they shared freely. They felt that by doing so, some of the problems in the pastorate could be dealt with and perhaps solved. To all of you, my heartfelt thanks! This is truly your book.

I am also indebted to the scores of pastors, their wives, and their children whom I have conversed with and observed during our years in the ministry. Many of them have unknowingly made important contributions.

Thanks must go, also, to the various churches who let me use rooms to hold interviews. Bethesda Hospital, Denver, also graciously offered me a room to use.

A project like this is never successful without a lot of prayer. Many people were praying with me and for me as I wrote, but I want to mention my special prayer partners, Diana Kirkevold, Sue Golladay, Terri Higgins, and Greta Foley, for their constant encouragement.

And then there is my long-suffering family, each one of whom played an important part. Lisa edited; Sharon, Mary Lee, and Sharon Watson typed; eleven-year-old Katherine did all the cooking and dishwashing during the final weeks of scrambling to meet the publisher's deadline.

My husband Henry's help is harder to describe. From the beginning—three and a half years before the manuscript was finally finished—he encouraged me to begin and suggested ways to do it. He also carefully read each chapter as it was completed and often offered further suggestions. We completely talked through a couple of the difficult chapters before I wrote anything down. After twenty-one years of constant dialogue, our thinking has been formed by each other to such an extent that it would be nearly impossible for either of us to produce anything that was not influenced by the other. So, to Henry, a most profound thank you.

I also want to thank my parents for a wonderful Christian home and the Christian Reformed Church for a marvelous heritage of commitment to marriage and the family.

Chapter 1

The Casualties

Karen

Nervous, taut, at times holding her emotions in check by a tremendous act of her will—then losing the narrow edge of control and taking some moments to weep, and once again getting a grasp of her composure—slowly, and with great pain, the tiny, attractive woman told me her story. And an incredible story it was! For the last four years she had lived with her husband as his wife, raised their children, run the parsonage, and every Sunday had listened to him preach, all the while knowing that he was living with another woman!

Gently, carefully, I asked questions, trying to sort out useful information from the complicated, sordid mess her marriage had become. She was quite willing to talk to me, in spite of the pain, because she hoped that by sharing her experience others might be helped. "If only one marriage would be saved," she cried, "only one couple spared the heartache I've gone through, it would be worth it." So for a couple of hours she talked, cried, and talked some more.

She had never wanted to be a minister's wife. In fact, before she consented to marry her husband she had asked him if there were any chance of his becoming a minister. Since he had gone to a Bible college, she thought perhaps the ministry was a possibility. She wanted to be sure that he understood she felt no calling to be a minister's wife. So they were laymen for the first seven years of their marriage. Later, when he felt called to the ministry, she had a real struggle. She agonized in prayer, feeling that she would be a real stumbling block to her husband if she were to resist, yet having a hard time accepting his decision. Finally she felt God was calling her as well as her husband. She would be a pastor's wife.

For several years all went well. After seminary her husband took a pastorate and the Lord blessed his work. He became a successful preacher immediately. His personal magnetism was a great help in teaching, preaching, and counseling. Their marriage was blessed with four beautiful children. Everything seemed to be in order.

With the 20/20 vision that hindsight gives, she later realized that much of his "success" in the ministry was an inordinate drive to feed his tremendously insecure ego. He pushed himself unmercifully, working constantly, and thriving on the praise and recognition he received. However, when anyone criticized the church or the Lord's work in any way, he took it as a personal affront. His self-esteem would once again be wounded.

Perhaps another aspect related to his pastoral failure was his insistence on doing all visiting and counseling alone. Often she would ask to accompany him on a sick call or another simple visit, but always she was rebuffed. Even when calling on strangers in the community he would never take a partner. When on occasion his elders offered to go with him, their offers were politely but firmly declined.

He seemed to be particularly gifted in helping women. His reputation as a counselor grew. So it is perhaps not very surprising that eventually he became deeply involved emotionally with one of the women he was counseling. This level of emotional intimacy led quickly to physical intimacy.

The affair went on for four years, hidden, strangely enough, from everyone *but* his wife. Though one or two others may have suspected that all was not right, no one but his wife actually knew what was going on. Finally he resigned from the ministry, but never submitted a reason. After divorcing his wife, the four-year affair fizzled out and he eventually married still another woman.

Today he is a successful salesman, although those who know him say that he is a very unhappy man. He no longer attends church, and he seems to take a perverse pleasure in drinking, gambling, and other pursuits which he formerly preached against.

Through those four agonizing years when she alone lived with her awful secret, this former pastor's wife told me that at one time she thought she was losing her mind, and at another time she seriously considered suicide.

Though obviously deeply scarred, she seems to have begun putting her life back together. She is working full time and has started to see friends again after avoiding all friends and acquaintances for over a year.

God has sustained and blessed her children also.

She told me that her children are a great blessing to her. She feels that they have been given a double portion of love for her to make up for the loss of her husband.

Edith

Edith's story is not so dramatic. There was no "other woman," no sudden wrenching away of a husband and father. Edith herself initiated the divorce, but she waited twenty-six years, until all three of her sons were grown and had made homes of their own. Even so, one of the boys had emotional difficulties for a time. Presently, however, all seem to be doing well, and one is even attending seminary and plans to be a minister.

Edith and her ex-husband are still on good terms. In fact, when she recently inherited some heirlooms and sold them, she shared the proceeds with John. She felt it was only fair, since he had supported her for so many years. They still have family gatherings occasionally where they both get together with their sons, daughters-in-law, and grandchildren. Neither of them has remarried, although Edith indicated that she would like to marry again. Since she is a well-groomed, young-looking woman with an easy smile, she has plenty of escorts.

While she talked, we drank tea and munched on the brownies she had baked for the occasion. As I listened and took notes, the reasons for the collapse of Edith's marriage were not immediately obvious to me. She and her ex-husband had both been raised thinking that divorce is wrong. Yes, they were still friendly. No, there had been no other women or other men involved. No, she had not been forced to be the leader of different societies in the church. Yes, she did some visiting with her husband—especially calling on the sick.

Then she started at the beginning. She and her husband had started to date when she was a junior in high school. He was her pastor at the time, and a good many years older than she. He was a very talented preacher—an excellent speaker. Edith was a good student and had always planned to go to college. But when the minister wanted to marry her, even her parents were won over. She now believes that if it had been anyone but the minister, her parents would never have given their blessing to such an early marriage for their daughter. Three weeks after her graduation from high school, when she was barely seventeen, she moved into the parsonage of a large city church in the east.

Since there was a good liberal arts college in their town, she enrolled for the fall term. But by that time she was pregnant and found the demands of home, church, and school to be too much for her. She dropped out soon after she started, and never did resume her formal education. Her husband, on the other hand, had several degrees when they were married, and he went on to get a doctor's degree and do a year of post-graduate study at different times during their marriage.

I asked about the stereotype of a minister's wife and whether she had felt the pressures of it. Edith answered that although she never felt pushed to take on any particular job in the church, she did feel guilty a lot of the time. It was not so much a matter of what she should do as what she should *be*. She felt that she was presenting a false front to the world. Everyone thought that because she was the pastor's wife she was, by definition, good, kind, and spiritual—things that she did not feel herself to be. And so she found herself playing a role—not on purpose, but by an accident of circumstance. She would have liked to be all the things people thought she was, but she didn't know how. And so she found herself pretending, without having made a conscious decision to do so. Her husband didn't seem able to help her. From the beginning there was never much serious communication between them.

Very early in the marriage she felt that she was in a trap from which she could not struggle free. Soon she stopped struggling. Sometimes she would go to bed during the day and simply stare at the walls. Intermittently she would take tranquilizers for short or long periods of time. Occasionally she would wonder to herself how marriage could be so terribly different from courtship. Looking back on those years, she realizes that she had a very low self-image. She didn't feel that her opinions counted for anything. In fact, her husband rarely, if ever, asked for her thinking on any aspect of the ministry.

I asked whether they had ever had any marriage counseling

when they knew that their marriage was in trouble. She answered that her husband would never discuss their getting counseling as a couple. He always considered it to be her problem. She indicated that if they had been able to get counseling during that first year, it might have helped a lot.

She became very close to her children. From the vantage point of many years after the fact, she believes that she probably spent a lot of time with the boys to escape an uncomfortable and increasingly unprofitable relationship with her husband. One result of this is that she still has very good relationships with all three of her sons.

Mike

Mike, a successful pastor in an inner-city congregation, shared the story of his marriage failure interspersed with his commentary on why it happened. He had taken a good look at himself and his situation and had come to some definite conclusions. He too had perfect vision after the fact and could point out many of the traps that he and his wife had fallen into.

In the racially mixed inner-city situation in which he was working, Mike found it very easy to get too involved. He explained to me that a minister in a minority congregation is a combination of mother-confessor, preacher, lawyer, folk doctor, and general sage. He would get many calls at all times of the day or night, and he always responded. He just wasn't home enough.

Then as his marriage began to deteriorate, his absences became a means of escape. This was never a conscious decision. It was just that as the tension between him and his wife increased, it became easier to take on more responsibilities that would keep him away from home. He accepted work on some national committees which enabled him to travel a lot. As he received more and more satisfaction (or "strokes" as he put it) from his increasing involvement in the community and from his travelling, his wife became increasingly more jealous and dissatisfied. Since she had never wholeheartedly accepted the people of the church, she had no real friends in the congregation.

One day when he returned from a trip, she simply wasn't there. She had taken the children and moved out.

Now she doesn't attend church at all. She is living with a man who has no hobbies or community involvement whatsoever. He works an eight-hour day and spends the rest of his time at home.

Ironically, he is also different from her ex-husband in another way. He has only an eighth-grade education, and he works as a janitor. She has a master's degree.

At the time I talked to Mike he felt that his work was going well. His self-image had pretty well recovered from the trauma of the divorce, and he was not unhappy. He had a good relationship with his three children, all teenagers. In fact, all of them were still in his church.

However, he was pretty pessimistic about the chances of finding another wife. He said that as soon as his dates would find out that he was a minister, their interest in him would suddenly cool.

On the other hand, his married pastor friends are constantly trying to play matchmaker. They set up dates for him and give him names of women he might be interested in. I suggested that perhaps they were just trying to be helpful. He disagreed. He was convinced that as a divorced man he was a definite threat to them. He represented what could happen to them.

One happy result of an unhappy situation is that Mike now finds himself in the role of counselor to many of his colleagues whose marriages are shaky. He says that they don't realize that their marriages are in trouble any more than he did. It's such a sneaky thing. He now alerts his fellow ministers to the danger signals.

On one occasion one of his friends told him that after a disagreement, his wife had gotten into the car and driven a hundred miles in the direction of her mother's house before turning back. The friend wondered whether this might be a sign of trouble developing. Mike told him that he was in trouble *right now* and had better move fast to save his marriage. The couple started counseling, and they were able to begin communicating. They learned to look at their problems and find solutions. Mike has been used in a number of other situations to help head off divorce among his colleagues.

Scott and Jan

The story of Scott's divorce was one of the saddest that I heard, because it seemed so unnecessary. There was no third person involved, no big crisis. In fact, by traditional standards their marriage had everything going for it.

Scott and Jan grew up in the same town and attended the same high school. They were the classic childhood sweethearts who dated for years and then got married. Their parents were friends. They knew the same people. They had interests in common. Their church background was nearly identical. He had seen her with her hair in rollers; she had seen him when he hadn't shaved. He knew she couldn't stand catsup on hamburgers; she knew how he liked his eggs. They accepted each other's foibles. It should have been a "perfect" marriage.

For quite a few years it seemed to be. Or at least it seemed so to Scott. Jan enjoyed keeping house and taking care of their five children. She enjoyed the busyness and entertaining that went with the parsonage. Their social calendar was full—often they were booked months in advance.

All this changed when Scott took a position as campus minister at a nearby college. Jan was no longer running a manse. She didn't really identify with students, so she didn't invite them over very often. Scott very much enjoyed his new work, but Jan could not share his enthusiasm. She felt as if she had lost part of her job.

Just at this point in her life a friend introduced her to Women's Lib. She started going to meetings and began yearning for the schooling she had dropped when she got married. She decided to go to business college in preparation for a career. After graduation she immediately began working full time outside her home.

Three years later she filed for divorce. By this time it seemed as if Scott and Jan were going in entirely different directions. Their working hours were such that they seldom had meals together. Neither was involved in the other's life except to bicker about the house or the children. When the tension seemed unbearable, she asked him to move out.

Scott does not seem to be bitter about what happened to his marriage. But as we talked it became apparent that he has been bewildered and hurt by others besides his wife. The first thing he mentioned was that from the time it became obvious that their marriage was in trouble up until the present, none of his colleagues has said a word. Not one of his minister friends, either in his denomination or in any other denomination, has offered any counsel or even a sympathetic ear. Friends who had gone all the way through college and seminary with him chose to totally ignore the break-up of his marriage, as if it weren't happening. No one offered to help. He feels a great loneliness.

The other baffling and disappointing aspect of the situation was the attitude of the counselors to whom his wife had talked. Over three years' time she had seen several different counselors, all of them Christians. While none of them told her that she should get a divorce, they all pointed out that it was one of her options. After she got over her initial repugnance, divorce seemed by far the most attractive of the alternatives. It seemed to be much easier than trying to rebuild a relationship which had seriously deteriorated.

As a pastor, Scott had always counseled against divorce. He firmly believed that the Bible taught reconciliation. He had assumed that other Christian counselors would hold the same beliefs. So he felt betrayed when he discovered the kind of advice his wife had been given.

Jackie and Dick

When I talked to Jackie she had been divorced for three years, and she was beginning to see her marriage and her ex-husband in a clearer perspective. Some things which had completely baffled her at first were starting to make a perverse kind of sense.

Jackie is a very capable person. During high school and college she won many trophies and awards for her speaking ability. She told me that this was the thing that attracted Dick to her in the first place. (My own observation is that this was probably not the only thing that attracted him. Jackie is still, in her fifties, a strikingly beautiful woman.)

For almost thirty years they worked together in the ministry, building several large congregations from nothing. Both of them were exceptionally gifted, and they poured their considerable energies into the work. Dick preached three times each Sunday, taught pastors' classes, conducted a jail ministry, counseled, visited, led young people's groups, supervised the construction of buildings, and often did carpentry work right along with the workmen. Jackie taught Sunday school, played for church services, sang in the choir, spoke for different Christian groups in the city, entertained almost nonstop, and raised their five children.

Although both of them worked extremely hard in the ministry, Dick was the pusher. He drove himself unmercifully, and he drove everyone around him as well. Jackie tells of having to go through with a dinner party while in labor. On another occasion she had major surgery and gave a speech to two thousand people the day after coming home from the hospital.

Although in a sense she was playing a role—doing what her husband wanted or what the congregation wanted, rather than what *she* thought she should do—she found a measure of happiness, because she was good at what she was doing, and everyone accepted her.

She also thought that she had a happy marriage, even though she felt a lack in the area of communication. But most of the time she was too busy to think about it.

Then one day she found out that her husband had been carrying on an affair for over a year with a woman in the church who was twenty years younger than he. Actually the board of directors and several other women in the church knew about it before Jackie did. When confronted, her husband denied everything; but a short time later he ran off with the woman. Jackie got in touch with him and told him she would do anything to save their marriage. They tried living together again for a while, which she described as "hell on earth."

After a short time he left and started divorce proceedings. The other woman also got a divorce so they could marry. For the woman it meant giving up her young children; for him it was the ministry.

In retrospect Jackie realizes that Dick always had a tremendous need for ego satisfaction. She believes the reason he drove himself so hard was that he craved praise for accomplishing so much. He preferred to do everything himself. He seldom delegated responsibility, except to her. She believes that he looked on her as an extension of himself.

Although he was basically a loner—he never in his life had a close friend—he needed the approval of people. He refused to visit with other ministers and their wives, but he loved leading young people's groups or women's groups. His charisma was especially apparent with women: all the women in the church loved him.

Jackie has obviously borne a great deal of pain through the whole ordeal—wrenching, tearing pain and humiliation. Yet I sensed that she still feels a certain love for her ex-husband. She pointed out that with the divorce she lost her husband, her home, her job, and her position in the community. But she has successfully dealt with her loss and the bitterness that accompanied it. She has regained a sense of her own worth and is secure in a new career. She seems as happy as one could expect in her situation. I sensed emotional and spiritual reserves which will continue to carry her on as she rebuilds her life.

Diane and Tony

When Diane heard that I was interviewing people in order to

write a book about pastors and their marriages, she was very eager to cooperate. She thought that if she and Tony had been given help earlier, things might have been different. She also hoped that by hearing her story some others might be spared going through the same agony. Finding a time for an interview was a problem, however. She was working away from home during the day, and after work some of the children were always around. We finally settled on a time when the last teenager was in bed: 11:00 p.m.

Head-over-heels in love, stars in her eyes, head in the clouds—any of these clichés would have aptly described Diane at the time of her marriage to Tony. She was a pretty, personable girl with many admirers, but none of the others stood a chance after she met Tony. He was also very attractive—a big bear of a man who was a star football player in college. He had a very outgoing personality and was well liked. He too could have had his choice of many girls to marry. Their friends considered it an ideal match.

Things went well for the first few years. Tony was a warm, understanding person. He and Diane had, in her words, "fantastic communication—a really terrific relationship." She was deeply in love with her husband and considered him to be as committed as she.

In his counseling, Tony was always insistent on husbands and wives reconciling. He believed that his job as a pastor was to help them resolve their differences and lead them back together. But when it happened to him, the rules didn't apply. The woman for whom he left Diane had come to him initially for counsel because of marital problems. She claimed that she had never found fulfillment in her marriage. According to Diane, this was a challenge for Tony. He had to show her what a relationship could really be like! When she became pregnant, he left his wife to marry her.

While Tony was having his affair, others in the church suspected that something was going on; but Diane never did. She trusted Tony. She said that she always had him on a pedestal.

When he left Diane he resigned from the ministry. He is now a longshoreman. He gives her a tiny child support check each month—about the equivalent of one week's rent. So she has to work outside her home.

Tony often comes to visit Diane and their five children. At first the children wanted nothing to do with him. Now, however, they aren't so angry anymore, just lacking respect for their father. The youngest child said it kindly. "I'm afraid Daddy won't go to heaven when he dies."

Tony tells Diane that he isn't happy and she knows that this is true. She is still in love with him and often wishes that she hadn't given him the divorce. She says he is a real "con man"—that he can charm anybody into doing what he wants. Yet I have the feeling that if he were free today, she would probably take him back, in spite of all the pain and trouble he has given her.

Gloria and John

As Gloria related her story, she kept stressing the fact that Christians are not immune to marriage problems. Nor are ministers and their wives. Because her divorce sneaked up on her, she tries to alert others to the fact that it can happen to them too. She shared with me that she can see serious problems developing between the young pastor and his wife in the church she is now attending. She is struggling with whether or not to offer them some help, and if so, how to go about it. She is sure that they are as unaware of what is happening to them as she was.

Gloria thought that her husband and she had a good relationship. They were honest and open in their communication. They seemed to have adjusted well to each other. They had five children, all of them wanted and planned-for. But her husband became involved with another woman and very suddenly left. She didn't even see him again for two years.

This was not a classic case of his becoming involved with a woman who was coming to him for counseling. She was not a member of the church. She was someone that he met at his job as a salesman. In addition to being a pastor, he was holding a second job in order to provide for his family. The church that he was serving was quite small and was financially unable to furnish an adequate salary for him and his family. So he was forced to moonlight. Gloria felt that the whole problem was a matter of his simply drifting away from God. God was no longer the focus of his life.

Eventually the other woman became John's second wife. Gloria finally gave him a divorce because she had had one nervous breakdown and was on the verge of another. She had no strength left, so she quit fighting. She figured that her marriage was hopelessly lost, so she gave it up.

Gloria said that she spent many hours agonizing over what she had done wrong or failed to do. Now that they are on speaking terms again, she has asked John what he thinks she did wrong. He always insists that she didn't fail—that the fault was all his. But she said she realizes that it always takes two to break up a marriage. She feels that part of the blame had to be hers.

One of the things that Gloria blames herself for is not recognizing the signs that indicated she and her husband were growing apart. The warning signals were there. She simply didn't read them. She was very involved in the church. He was busy with serving as a minister and with his job as a salesman. The things she was doing in the church didn't directly relate to his work as pastor and vice versa. Both of them were busy working in the church, but they weren't working together. While he was doing his pastoral work, she was coordinating suppers and such. Each was wrapped up in his own concerns, and they weren't taking the time to share them with each other. She realizes now that they should have made time to be alone together. They needed to get inside each other's minds, to share their feelings. Instead they each carried on separately. They lived together: they shared bed and board. But they were not really functioning as a couple. Neither one of them was putting any time or effort into their relationship. So in a sense it died from lack of nourishment—from simple neglect. She now encourages all her married friends to have "dates" with each other—times to get dressed up, go someplace, and really talk to each other. She tells them they can't afford *not* to, even if they have to pay a baby-sitter.

Another area in which Gloria senses blame is that of her personal appearance. She is basically a good-looking woman, but she gained a good deal of weight in the course of their marriage. She also failed to take enough interest in her hair and clothes so that she looked attractive. She became acutely conscious of her shortcomings in this area after she met John's new wife. Although several years older than John, she keeps herself very attractive. She is slim, well dressed, and she uses make-up skillfully. An irony here is that John always told Gloria that he didn't want her to wear fancy clothes and make-up. Yet this is obviously one of the things that attracted him to his second wife. Gloria does not put all the blame in this area on John, however. She feels that wives have an obligation to remain physically attractive for their husbands. She knew this, and she thinks all wives really know it. But some choose to ignore it. She believes that if the marriage is in good shape in other ways, it will not die because a wife neglects her looks. But she thinks that it definitely was an important factor in her case.

The thing that saddens her the most about her divorce is the effect that it has had on the children. She was forced to take an outside job almost immediately, since her husband simply disappeared and left her stranded. She had no way to support herself and her five children except by going out to the marketplace. The girls helped out by baby-sitting as soon as they were old enough, and the boys both had paper routes. They all pitched in, which was good for them.

But Gloria's job, the only job that she could find, took her away from the house most afternoons and evenings. So she was never home when the children came home from school. She couldn't greet them with cookies and milk and hear about their problems or triumphs the way she used to. In addition, she wasn't able to be home in the evenings to meet their friends and to set deadlines for them.

As the boys grew older, she suspected that they were running with the wrong crowd, but she felt helpless to do anything about it. She had a nagging notion in the back of her mind that all was not well with her sons. Yet it came as a terrible shock one day to discover that both of her boys were dealing in drugs. Since she could be counted on to be away, they had been using her home as a base of operations.

When I talked to her, some ten years after the breakup of her marriage, Gloria was very optimistic about her family. In spite of the terrible trauma that they went through for several years, she believes that God is redeeming the situation. She believes that He will keep His promise to be a father to the fatherless. The two older girls have made a commitment to Christ and are happily married to Christian men. The boys have both made a turnabout and are now serving the Lord. One is engaged to a Christian girl. The youngest child, a girl, is still having problems. Her life-style is decidedly non-Christian at the moment. She continues her involvement with a series of "wrong" men. But even so, Gloria has maintained a close relationship with her. She is confident that the Lord is dealing with this last child as He has with the others, and will bring her back to Him in His time.

Although the four oldest children are now living as Christians and the youngest shows signs of becoming open to the Lord, none has escaped unscathed. All bear deep scars. Each of the older girls had to work through a basic mistrust of men before she could establish a working relationship upon which to build a marriage. One was in her late twenties when she married; the other was in her early thirties. Gloria sees the Lord's hand in providing men for both of them who were patient and understanding while the girls struggled with their doubts about men and their fear of failure.

The boys have been deeply hurt as well. The older one was so angry because of what his father had done to his mother that he refused to see him at all for several years. He had had him on a pedestal because he was a minister. When his father came crashing down, Bill was devastated. Years later Bill confronted his father, still seething with anger. As a result they now see each other occasionally. The relationship is still strained, but Gloria feels she can see slow progress.

Gloria is now fifty-seven and has never remarried. She said that once she came close, but she got cold feet at the last minute. She's never found anyone else she'd like to marry.

Lisa and Steve

Lisa was the only ex-wife I talked to who seemed to have no regrets about the breakup of her marriage. Although she was the one who initiated the divorce proceedings, she told me that she never felt bad about it. And since that time she has never wondered whether she did the right thing.

As she sat talking to me about her husband and the other woman whom she described as a "sex bomb," it was difficult to think of anyone much sexier than Lisa herself. Looking at her tall and curvy figure, the word "lush" came to mind. With her long black hair and expressive blue eyes, she somewhat resembled a young Elizabeth Taylor.

Finding out about the other woman was perhaps not as much of a shock for Lisa as for some other wives, because she knew her marriage was in trouble long before the affair began. She and Steve had even gone for counseling once or twice, but hadn't followed through with it. She didn't dare to let anyone else know that the marriage was shaky. She felt that as a minister's wife she had an image to maintain.

Lisa had very little good to say about her ex-husband. Perhaps the hurt was still too new—our interview was only some months after she had found out about his infidelity.

According to her, Steve had a Dr. Jekyll and Mr. Hyde personality. She claimed he had real presence in the pulpit and was charming to people in the congregation as well as to his colleagues. To everyone but his family, in fact. At home he was an obsessive, critical, angry person. He was home as little as possible, and when he was home he wouldn't talk very much. He would hide behind a book or in front of the TV.

He ignored his three children and his wife equally. She claims that the children, who are eight, five, and three years old, don't really miss their daddy because they never knew him very well. Lisa tried to talk about his work with him at different times, but never succeeded. Whenever she would offer any idea, he would refuse it. He would preach good sermons on marriage and she felt like saying, "Try it at home!"

From the beginning of the marriage Steve criticized her: the way she dressed, her housekeeping, the way she entertained. She came to the conclusion that he didn't love her—that he never really had loved her. She thinks that she fit the requirements that he had for a wife: she was attractive, intelligent, a college graduate, and from the right part of the country. He felt that she would serve his purposes and project the right image, so he set out to get her. Lisa thinks that the ministry was an ego trip for him, and she was part of the trip.

At the time we had our interview, Steve was trying to get her to consider reconciliation. But she would have none of it. She was sure that he wasn't sincere, that he was only making a gesture to try to keep from being deposed. She told me that at the same time he was trying to get her to take him back, he was spreading gossip about her. Every time she would talk to a mutual friend, she would hear something else ugly that he had said about her. So she came to the conclusion that he had not repented and was not willing to make an honest effort toward rebuilding their marriage.

During our talk I asked Lisa my usual questions about the stereotype of a pastor's wife. She said that she hadn't felt an undue amount of pressure in this area, and wasn't really sick of being a minister's wife. She was only sick of being *this* minister's wife.

To answer my question about living in a parsonage, Lisa said that she thought the situation might have been different if she and Steve had owned their own home. Then he would have had to do a certain number of things around the house, so he wouldn't have been able to be gone all the time. Perhaps then he would have been with the children more, too.

Lisa also has some firm ideas about pastors counseling women alone. Steve's affair fit the classic "minister goes to bed with attractive counselee" pattern. Their first session lasted four hours. From the start he made appointments for her several times a week, and she would call him on the phone between sessions. What amazed Lisa was that as the affair progressed, they were not the least bit discreet. Steve would park his car right in front of his paramour's house for hours at a time. But when confronted, he lied about the relationship to everyone, including the members of the board of trustees.

When we talked about remarriage, Lisa said that there was no man in her life at the moment. But it was clear that she intended to remarry eventually. And I was quite sure that having set remarriage as one of her goals, she would have little trouble accomplishing it.

George

George is one of the men who has survived divorce without losing his ministerial status. There was no infidelity on his part. His wife left him.

When I talked to George, his divorce was several years behind him. He was happily remarried to a woman whose situation was very similar to his: her husband had left her.

He had some very definite ideas about what had gone wrong with his first marriage and was taking specific steps to avoid these pitfalls with his new wife. Even though his first wife had been unfaithful to him, he was willing to take the lion's share of blame for the breakup of their marriage.

George talked about the pressures on a minister and his wife, especially when they are just starting out. He said that in the first two or three years the pastor is very insecure about his role. Even though he is ordained, people keep saying, "You're going to be a good minister someday." So he feels that he has to prove himself. He pushes himself to do as much as possible, and he begins to put pressures on his wife as well. Obviously the more she does in the church, the more it will help to get him established. So both the pastor and his wife find themselves having to do things without choosing to do them themselves.

Also, at the same time that the ministry is a new experience for the couple, in most cases their marriage is new as well. So they aren't mature as individuals, and their marriage is not yet secure. They are often still at the point of finding their marriage style—of trying to fit the odd pieces of their relationship into a well-ordered whole.

This combination of handicaps can be disastrous. In their case it was. In their first church, a small country congregation, she was very involved and enjoyed it. But two years later they moved to a church with a thousand members. There was a gradual building up of tension. It was just taken for granted that she would do different jobs in the church. She no longer felt like a real person. To use her own word, she felt like baggage. George said that she is a natural leader, but she didn't find a chance to exercise her gifts. She was very busy, but she was busy simply performing a lot of chores. She didn't feel that her real talents were being tapped. In addition, she felt that she wasn't getting enough attention from her husband. So she looked for, and found, masculine attention elsewhere.

George says that his divorce and remarriage drastically altered his priorities. Where previously the demands of the ministry were allowed to push out anything and everyone else, now his family comes first. He now sees being a Christian husband and father as his calling and considers the ministry to be his job.

He also realizes that a minister must make his wife feel that he loves her for herself, not for what she is doing. One of the specific steps which he has taken is to regularly schedule dates with his wife. He writes these dates down on his calendar along with his other appointments.

He blocks off certain segments of time to spend with her. If something or someone else tries to claim one of these blocks of time, he simply says that he has a commitment.

This policy has not been a problem for the congregation. George has found that people will demand of you what you let them. If you set limits, they will stay within them.

Maggie and Tom

Maggie is convinced that her husband's deep involvement in psychology was the undoing of her marriage. She and Tom had been married for several years and things were going well in the church and at home. Then Tom started getting heavily involved in awareness groups, encounter groups—all sorts of group dynamics meetings.

At first Maggie attended some of the meetings with him. However, her initial uneasiness gave way to downright disapproval as she became more aware of their methods and practices. She considered that a lot of what they were doing was contrary to Scripture. So she refused to participate further and told her husband exactly why.

She pleaded with Tom to quit going as well, but he wouldn't listen. He seemed to be hooked. Not only did he go to the meetings. He also read a great many books recommended by group members: books on hypnotism and other more esoteric subjects.

These groups would probe into whether or not he loved his father and mother, his wife, and all the other people close to him. He would come home in tears after many of the sessions. Finally he decided that he did *not* love his wife; he initiated divorce proceedings.

Maggie said that she saw a gradual but very marked change in Tom's personality from the time of his first involvement with these groups. And since she would not change in the same way, their marriage came to the breaking point.

The divorce seemed to Maggie almost like a male menopause reaction. A few months after the divorce he remarried someone younger, but Maggie doesn't think he's very happy. He keeps calling her and coming over to the house. Even after he was married he wanted her to go out on dates with him. She thinks he is still very mixed-up.

Wes and Donna

The one thing that Wes blames most for the breakup of his marriage is that both he and his wife bought the idea that the ministry came first and the family after. They never built a relationship—they were too busy building a parish. If Wes were to do it over, he would insist on privacy—on keeping the marital relationship apart from the church. He became quite vehement when he talked about "this business" of hiring one person and getting two. He heatedly explained that when a hospital or clinic hires a doctor, it doesn't get a receptionist thrown in free. And a factory doesn't get a man's wife along with the man who was hired. He added that the Lord doesn't say that a minister has to serve with greater intensity than anyone else, either.

Wes went on to say that in the parsonage he and his wife lived as if their home belonged to everyone. People would walk in any time without even knocking, and he and Donna would make them feel welcome. They never had any real privacy, either for the two of them, or as a family.

The kids resented this. They didn't like the idea that they never knew who might come barging in. They wanted respect for their privacy. Wes thinks that his kids are glad to be out from under the pressure of living in the parsonage. People had different expectations for them as minister's children than they had for other people's kids.

Wes did admit that adultery was involved in his divorce. He "stepped out on" his wife, as he put it. But he claims that his affair did not break up the marriage. The involvement with another woman was only short-lived. Wes did not seem to place much significance on his infidelity. As he talked, I thought that it would be interesting to see whether his wife were as casual about it as he.

Wes resigned from the ministry when his marriage broke up. He now sounds rather bitter about the ministry. He claims that he couldn't really see himself "doing the parson bit" for the rest of his life. He felt that he was in a straitjacket. He didn't want other people to tell him how to live, or what to think.

He no longer believes that there is a "set of absolutes" as far as the faith is concerned. He says he could not continually try to explain what God thinks "as if we know what God is." He didn't have certain subjects settled in his own mind, so he couldn't preach on them. He claims that the ministry leaves no room for uncertainties or doubts. Now he attends church only infrequently. When he does go, it is to a large church of a denomination very different from the one in which he pastored.

He added that the more rigid the subculture, the more the pressures on a minister. He was pastoring a congregation in a small town in the deep south, where the community was a tight little entity. He thinks that if he had been living in California, for example, things might have been different.

He also talked about how the clergy are underpaid, which, he said, promotes a kind of masochism. They're surrounded on every side by affluence, yet they can't share in it. So they wear the hair shirt of poverty. He claimed that he is presently making four times as much money as he did in the ministry.

An insight which Wes contributed, which was not in answer to any of my queries, was that the ministry can be a real ego trip. He said that it was partly that for him. He kept getting stroked or "pounded on the back," as he put it. He experienced this as a response to a human need to put certain people on pedestals. A problem with this, according to Wes, is that some ministers actually come to believe that they are idols. Another problem he sees is that along with the need to have idols is the need to "clean house and destroy the idols." He indicated that living on a pedestal is a decidedly precarious business.

The impression I was left with after our interview was that Wes was not as happy with his present life-style as he would have me believe. He protested too much.

Paula and Bob

The picture that Paula painted of her ex-husband was that of an insecure man with both emotional and spiritual problems. She is two and a half years older than he, and this bothered him. He would always try to give the impression that he was older. She wasn't sure why this was so important to him. Also, she has a master's degree, and Bob has only three years of college. He served in a denomination which does not require college and seminary for ordination. The fact that she had more education than he mattered very much to him. Paula said that status was a big consideration for Bob.

A basic problem that Bob had—the problem which finally led to his resignation from the ministry—was that he was not honest. He always colored things to make himself look good. He got away with this for quite a while, simply because he was the minister. People assumed that he was telling the truth. When it looked as if he had not been totally honest in a given situation, everyone assumed that there had been a misunderstanding somewhere. But after a while it became apparent what was going on. Finally Bob got himself in way over his head in a situation and told a series of outrageous lies to try to extricate himself. It didn't work. He found himself caught in the tangled web of his own spinning. When he realized that he was no longer fooling the members of the board of directors and others with whom he worked, he immediately left the ministry and the church.

Bob has not gone to church since. About five years after his leaving the ministry, Paula divorced him. He is now remarried and living in Hawaii. His second wife is not a Christian.

Paula told me that she found out later that Bob had been unfaithful to her several different times during their nineteen-year marriage. Many of these affairs had occurred while he was in the ministry. He often counseled single women, and he usually counseled alone. He would never let his wife come with him. She said that in these situations she often felt like an outsider, but she would try to shove her feelings aside. She wanted to be a good wife, and she wanted to trust her husband.

Bob was very attracted to good-looking women. He would always seek them out for conversation, whether it was at a church function or a social gathering. Often when he was talking to an attractive woman, Paula would come up to them and they would both freeze. This bothered her. She began to wonder what it was that they were discussing, since they obviously could not continue talking about it in front of her.

Another problem area in their marriage was the matter of priorities. Paula said that she was last on Bob's list—after the church, his parents, and the children. She never got the time alone with him that she wanted and which she felt that they needed. His parents lived nearby, and he would see them regularly. He spent some time with the children, although they had to be squeezed in after his job responsibilities and after his time with his parents. They never had family devotions, even though Paula often pleaded with Bob about it.

We talked about living in a parsonage. Paula said that the house itself was never a problem. She didn't mind living in a house which the church owned. It was usually kept in good repair and was adequate for their needs.

The aspect of being in the parsonage which *did* bother her was that she and her children were always under scrutiny. She felt that she was living in a glass house. She was expected to set an example with her family. Also, she was not allowed to wear make-up or earrings. She was supposed to dress very conservatively. Again, this was so that she would be an example for the other women in the church. However, she noticed that her husband seemed to appreciate make-up and jewelry on other women, and he didn't appear to object to their more stylish clothes.

Paula said that being on display wouldn't have been so difficult if she had felt her husband's support. But she always felt that her problems were her own. Instead of encouraging her in her role, he added to her difficulties. He imposed as many of the restrictions on her as the congregation did.

She added that at the time she thought Bob was very successful as a pastor. But she has since found out that he wasn't nearly as effective as she had thought.

Marcie and Bill

Six feet tall, slender, and strikingly good looking, Marcie looked like a *Vogue* model. Actually, modelling had never entered her mind. She had wanted to be a minister's wife for as long as she could remember. With this in mind, she entered a Bible college after graduating from high school. She attended the college for two and a half years, and then quit to marry a minister whom she had met there.

As she told me the story of her wedding, I listened with a mixture of surprise, shock, and anger. Marcie's folks did not want them to get married. They didn't approve of Bill—didn't think he was right for her. Marcie said that he has always been a fighter, a debater. They quarreled a lot during their courtship. Her parents were uneasy about this. They thought it would only get worse after they were married.

Marcie did think that it would be a good idea to get premarital counseling. So she asked her pastor. He said that they didn't need it. After all, Bill was a pastor himself. Then she asked an old-time friend—the minister who was going to marry them. He gave her the same answer. So Marcie continued her preparations for the wedding.

At the last minute, after the showers had been given, the wedding details all completed, and the invitations mailed, she really panicked. She went again to talk with the minister who was to marry them. He refused to share her alarm. He told her that she just had the pre-wedding jitters.

So they were married. Marcie cried all through the ceremony. She said that the minister refused to look her in the eye the whole time. Everyone else simply assumed that her tears were tears of happiness.

Marcie and Bill didn't sleep together on their wedding night, and in the morning she called her parents. They told her that they would come to get her. They said that it wasn't too late to back out—that she could get an annulment. But she decided that it wouldn't be fair to all the people who had been involved in the wedding and all the guests who had attended. She decided that she should go through with it.

From that very shaky beginning, things did not get a great deal better. Bill and Marcie had trouble all during the ten years of their marriage. Marcie claims that people could just look at them and tell that they had problems.

For one thing, they were both role-playing. Bill is a terrific speaker. He was always very successful from the pulpit. He called door-to-door and counseled. He did all the things a pastor is supposed to do. But Marcie says that he was selling himself. He is a super salesman. In fact, now that he has left the ministry he has become a sales executive.

Marcie, too, did all the required things. She had her life exceptionally well organized. She had people in the house at all hours, yet her housework always got done. She sang solos with the church choir. She spoke for different groups. She went to conferences.

But in all of this church work, instead of complementing each other, they were constantly competing. Both are natural leaders and strong personalities. Marcie said that she knew she should be submissive and so she tried, but she never managed it.

They always had a problem communicating. They never seemed to really talk things out. On his day off he never took her anywhere. He would play golf or go off somewhere else without her. Often when Marcie was conversing at a dinner party, Bill would give her a sharp kick under the table. This was his way of telling her to shut up. He would sometimes even cut her down from the pulpit. She went to psychiatrist after psychiatrist during their marriage, in an attempt to see whether she was the problem and if so, what to do about it.

Another problem which was not the root of their trouble, but contributed to it, was their continual financial struggle. They never had an adequate salary. This became another area of tension and conflict. They were always hassling about where the money should go, and they tended to accuse each other of spending too much. Actually she thinks neither of them was extravagant. It was simply a matter of not enough paycheck to go around.

Marcie had another complaint which I became familiar with in talking to ex-ministers' wives: her husband would always counsel and call alone. He would never take her with him. He visited members of the congregation by himself, and he went knocking on doors by himself. He did not want his wife along. He went so far as to bring people to the house and tell Marcie to leave.

In a typical case of ministerial adultery, Bill became involved with a woman whom he was counseling. He met her for the first time when he was calling door-to-door. She eventually became a member of the church. In fact, she and Marcie became friends. She would often baby-sit the children when Marcie wanted to attend a seminar or a conference. Since Marcie had twins and a toddler just fifteen months younger, she looked on this woman as a real godsend. The days off gave her time to catch her breath a bit.

The irony of the situation was that by the time this woman became the children's stepmother, they were quite used to her. They had already gotten accustomed to her as a substitute mother.

Finally Bill and his paramour each divorced his respective spouse. Bill gave up the ministry to marry her. The woman gave up custody of her three small children to marry him. Her ex-husband has since moved to another part of the country, so she sees them only rarely. Marcie's comment at this point was that the wages of sin can be high.

One point in this case that I found to be very interesting was that Bill's conservatism was not only theological. Marcie described him as very strict. He was also, and still is, extremely conservative politically, as is his second wife. He often travelled around the country speaking for different ultra-conservative groups.

Marcie's life at this point seems well under control. She has a satisfying job, no financial worries, and a good social life. She is still young and very attractive. She is in no hurry to find another husband. At this point her life is full. But should she decide she would like to marry again, my guess is that she would have no trouble finding suitors.

Mary Lou

Mary Lou's husband had been out of the ministry for five years when I talked to her, and they had been separated almost as long. She had adjusted quite well to being a single parent and to her role as one of the formerly married. However, coping with the twin shocks of losing a husband and losing her job as minister's wife had not been easy.

She had been very committed to her husband. When she became aware of his unfaithfulness to her the first time, they talked about it and she forgave him. Then he had an affair with one of the women in the church. The board of directors found out about it and he broke it off. He swore to Mary Lou that this woman really didn't mean anything to him, and she believed him. Then she caught him in a series of affairs, all of which he denied. Finally he abruptly quit the ministry. He did this while she was out of town for a few days after finding out about another affair.

Since then he has gone from woman to woman, always denying the affairs. Mary Lou thinks that none of them mean anything to him. It seems that anyone of the feminine gender will do, from wait-

resses and airline stewardesses whom he has never met before, to acquaintances of long standing. It appears to be almost a compulsion with him. The number of women who are available for this sort of thing still amazes her. It also makes her a little cynical.

Mary Lou still speaks very fondly of her husband. Although they have been separated all this time, she has not divorced him. She thinks he is telling the truth when he says that he still loves her and wants her back. She would like to take him back, in spite of all that he has put her through. But until she sees a repentance, she does not dare. She wouldn't be able to cope with his continual unfaithfulness and dishonesty.

As well as being committed to her husband, Mary Lou was also very committed to the ministry. Looking back on it, she thinks that she was always more committed to the work than her husband was. She enjoyed being in the parsonage. She loved having people in all the time, entertaining them and ministering to them. She felt that she was doing important work, and that she was doing it for the Lord.

She did say that their children weren't always as enthusiastic as she was about people being in their home all the time. They didn't feel that they really had any privacy, because they never knew when someone would come in.

When we became specific about the physical demands on a pastor's wife, Mary Lou said that there were times when she should have said "no" to meetings in their house. There was no particular reason why these meetings had to be in the parsonage. They could just as well have been held in different homes. She said that all this entertaining became a strain, and she should have had the gumption to say so.

Since her husband's adultery was the factor that precipitated their separation and also his leaving the ministry, we talked a bit about the minister and the "other woman." Mary Lou's insight into this phenomenon was that a minister with a weak ego feeds on women with problems. The attenton that each woman gives him bolsters his sagging self-image for a time. But it's never enough, because of course no one else can really give someone a sense of his own worth. So he is never satisfied, and he goes from one woman to the next, wherever he can get large doses of flattery and attention. Sometimes this includes sex, sometimes not.

While we were talking about this, Mary Lou volunteered the information that during the time that she's been separated from her husband, three ministers have offered to go to bed with her. She said they actually assumed that they would be doing her a favor since she was no longer living with her husband. These were all married men. She was both insulted and quite shocked. She would not have thought it strange if non-Christians had tried to seduce her. But she was not prepared to have to handle being propositioned by these supposedly happily married ministers. Even though her own minister husband had been unfaithful to her, she did not expect to find the problem to be so widespread. And it was particularly unsettling to have the very people that she was looking to for guidance and support turn out, instead, to be part of the problem.

Chapter 2

Ministerial Dropouts

The casualties we have been discussing so far have been marriage casualties. Most often when the marriage is shattered, the man is lost to the ministry as well. So they become double casualties.

However, there are some, particularly those whose wives left them instead of the other way around, who are able to continue in the ministry. Often their ministry does not appear to be impaired. Although in some ways it is a detriment, in other ways, particularly in certain counseling situations, the experience can be a plus factor. So it often seems to balance out somewhat. These men, however, never emerge unscarred. Divorce always exacts a toll.

I did not encounter any men who left their wives to marry other women while yet remaining in the ministry. Perhaps there are a certain number of these men around the country. But from my research, I would expect them to be a definite minority. Obviously adultery leading to divorce does not create the most compatible climate for effective ministry.

There is another kind of casualty in the ministry which does not include the breakup of a marriage, although the health of the marriage may be a large or even controlling factor in it. This type of casualty is the ministerial dropout. Every year scores of men leave the ministry, including the priesthood. Someone has said that Catholic priests leave the priesthood to get married, while Protestant ministers leave the ministry to get divorced. It usually doesn't solve their problem in either case.

It is extremely difficult to get statistics on the cases in which men leave the ministry due to pressure from their wives, because, understandably, these men are unwilling to implicate their marriages or their marriage partners. If a man were to publicize the fact that he was leaving the ministry to save a faltering marriage, that might very well be the final blow which would precipitate divorce. After all, what woman wants to be blamed for making her husband give up his profession?

Pastors are leaving the ministry for a number of reasons, of course, as Andre Bustanoby has pointed out in his informative article "Why Pastors Drop Out" in the January 7, 1977, issue of *Christianity Today*. There is the matter of low salaries. Hand in hand with the money problem is the problem of "the feeling of low professional worth." Only a generation ago the minister was usually the most educated person in the community besides being thought of as a "man of the cloth"—God's special representative. Today we have specialists who are trained to do almost all the different parts of the pastor's job. Psychologists, professional counselors, evangelists and teachers all speak, minister, and offer seminars in their areas of proficiency, each gaining a following. So the pastor may leave the ministry because his salary is not adequate, and he doesn't feel that he is particularly effective or necessary anyway. However, I know of several cases in which the wives were very unhappy in the parsonage and their husbands finally left the ministry to become teachers, musicians, or counselors. But saving the marriage was never the reason given for making the change. We will probably never know how many men have left the ministry for other professions because their marriages were in trouble.

Ralph Heynen, who has counseled hundreds of pastors and their wives in almost thirty years as chaplain in a Christian psychiatric hospital, says, "The variety and intensity of work required of the modern clergyman demand much of his energy and time. Often this leads to the neglect of his family. . . . The pastor's wife and children, too, have needs that must be met. They have no pastor to whom they can go; they have only an absentee huband and father. A number of the drop-outs from the ministry have resulted from the choice made by a pastor's wife, rather than first of all the choice of her husband."[4]

Chapter 3

The Walking Wounded: Ministers

So far we have talked about the casualties in the parsonage—complete disasters in which either the ministry or the marriage was lost. Often a man's ministry and marriage were bound up together and so were ruined together.

Most pastors manage to hang on to both their professions and their wives, but seldom without sustaining some trauma along the way. Sometimes their difficulties are relatively minor; often they are severe. These ministers are the ones which I call the "walking wounded."

Probably the most important difficulty which a minister has to deal with is discouragement. Even the pastors who seem most successful in their work admit that discouragement is always lurking in a corner nearby, waiting to catch them unawares.

Unreasonable Job Description

There are many things that contribute to this discouragement. A big factor is the size of the job. Although the formal demands of the job may seem fair enough, the actual demands on the pastor are usually multiplied many times over those outlined in the job description contained in a letter of call or an ordination form for the ministry. One form which I have before me, for instance, states that the duties of the minister are to "present to the people the Word of the Lord" as it applies to different situations, "instruct the children of the church in . . . doctrine . . . visit the members of the congregation . . . and comfort the sick." He is also to conduct worship services, including administering the sacraments and to "keep the church . . . in good discipline."[5]

Now this sounds like a reasonable job description. According to this a pastor would spend his time studying for and preparing his sermons, preaching and administering the sacraments, teaching doctrine classes and visiting the church members—especially the sick or those who need admonishing. This could nicely fit into a working week, particularly if the congregation were not too large. From what I have heard and read, most ministers a generation or two ago did just that, with the addition of conducting the weddings and funeral services of members of the congregation when the occasion arose, and acting as chairman of the church's governing body.

Any pastor entering the ministry today would smile at this list of duties. And he would have to be exceedingly naive to pattern his work solely on the basis of this job description. To do so would mean sure disaster. This ministerial job description can perhaps be best described as quaint. In fact, while reading through it I felt a rush of nostalgia for our first charge, a well-established congregation housed in a new building set down in the middle of the prairie. But that was long ago and in another country. Things have since changed in that congregation as well.

Evangelism

Let's examine the list again. The most obvious lack is in the area of evangelism. I suspect that when the form was written evangelism was hardly talked about, much less encouraged or practiced by the average pastor and congregation. Mostly it was left up to the few specialists who travelled from place to place holding revivals. Robert Schuller, James Kennedy, and the church growth people—all were part of the yet undreamed-of future. With a few exceptions, churches were pretty much content to take care of their own members. Like the Old Testament Jews, they would let others join the fellowship if they desired and if they showed that they were sincere. But not much effort toward recruitment was made. Churches were built on the location which best suited the convenience of the existing members. No thought was given to outreach when the land was being selected. Congregations were content to remain the same size indefinitely.

Today things have not changed much in many congregations as

far as actual lay involvement in evangelism is concerned. Unfortunately, many congregations do little more than talk about it. They leave the actual practice of evangelism to the minister and, usually, his wife. But talk about it they do. They realize that it must be done, and they expect the pastor to do it. Everyone wants the church to be growing, and it's the minister's responsibility to see to it that it is.

Other congregations have come to the point where they realize that evangelism is the whole church's business—that all the members must be involved. Even so the minister is invariably expected to give leadership in this area, both by teaching and by example. This involves much time spent in setting up a workable program, training the people, and often doing one-on-one evangelism himself for many hours a week.

Counseling

A second large area of the pastor's work not even mentioned in the form for ordination from which I quoted is counseling. When that form was originally composed, divorce was quite uncommon in the country as a whole, and much more uncommon in the church. Within the particular denomination for which the form was written, divorce was virtually nonexistent. Values were shared by all members of the family and passed on from one generation to the next. In most cases communities shared the same values as well. God, home, and country were not questioned. The Protestant work ethic was in full force. The Vietnam war, the hippie movement, and personal identity crises were all still in the future. When someone had a problem, his friends and neighbors did not always give him perfect advice; but at least they had a common fund of experience and shared values from which to draw.

Today, by contrast, in most places not only are there no values which the community holds in common, but often the community itself has all but disappeared. Webster defines "community" as "a unified body of individuals as (for example): people with common interests living in a particular area, or a group linked by a common policy." By that definition there are a great many people today who belong to no community at all. They have no one who shares their experiences and understands their problems. Friends and relatives are often far away.

As a society we have become so mobile that often our extended families are scattered all over the country. My husband and I, for example, live in the state of Washington. Our brothers and sisters are as far away as Georgia, Arizona, Michigan, Ontario and Nova Scotia. Though we do talk by long-distance telephone occasionally, and try to see each other every few years, obviously we aren't of much help to each other in our day-to-day problems. Only when there is a genuine crisis do we manage the plane fare to be of assistance to each other. And our situation is not unique.

This disappearance of common values coupled with the phenomenon of fragmented families means that there are many, many people with problems and no obvious place to turn for help. A great many of these people, whether or not they are members of a church, turn to the nearest or most convenient minister. There are two simple reasons for this: the minister is handy and, perhaps most important, there is no fee for professional services rendered.

So the pastor must, singlehandedly, try to deal with the personal problems of many of the members of his congregation in addition to trying to counsel a number of nonmembers. Since each counseling session typically takes an hour, and many of these people have weekly sessions, a great deal of the pastor's time can be taken up in this way. I suppose that the amount of time per week that a pastor spends on counseling depends on his gifts and on the circumstances of his parishioners. But I dare say that there is hardly a pastor serving a congregation anywhere today who would say that counseling does not take up a considerable share of his time.

Head Executive

Another change that has occurred in the church in recent years is that it has come to be run like a business. The elders, deacons, or members of the board tend to act as executives, with the minister being, in effect, the senior executive. So in spite of the fact that he has had no training in management, the pastor finds himself in a managerial position. If the church which he is pastoring is a large one, or even medium-sized, this can be a formidable task. He is in charge of setting up numerous committees and seeing that they function properly. Often he lacks the executive skills to properly delegate responsibility, so in the end he is stuck with jobs that he wasn't meant to do. And in any case, as the senior executive, the final responsibility for seeing that decisions are implemented is his. Harry Truman was well aware of this aspect of the presidency. He had a sign on his desk which read, "The buck stops here." The same thing is true of the pastor. Whether he likes it or not, whether he is equipped to handle it or not, the buck stops with him.

Outside Speaking

In addition to the many aspects of his job as pastor, the minister is usually regarded as a readily available public speaker in the community. Graduation exercises, eagle scout ceremonies, commemorative dinners, and young peoples' banquets all require speakers. Even small women's study groups find that their attendance is boosted when they can advertise an "outside speaker" for a special meeting. And when people are looking for a speaker, they often ask the same question which they ask when they are looking for a counselor: Who is available whom we won't have to pay? The answer is the same in both cases: a nearby minister.

Actually there is a slightly different twist to the answer in the case of the speaker. The *nearest* minister will often not do, because he is one's own and therefore too familiar. So the Presbyterian minister speaks for the Methodist women's group, the Methodist pastor speaks for the Congregationalists, and so forth. Or the local Presbyterian man addresses a group at a dinner at the Presbyterian church in the next town.

Although none of this outside speaking is actually part of the pastor's job, he finds it very difficult to decline these invitations. So this load is added to his already overfull schedule.

Besides speaking at different functions, the pastor often feels that he should be involved in other ways in the community, by membership in a service club, or perhaps by serving on the local school board. After all, as a leader he should be giving an example of good citizenship. Not only do others often assume he will do these things. He himself feels that he should.

Moonlighting

With the exception of some teachers, ministers are probably the only professional people in the United States today who hold two jobs out of necessity. One has a hard time imagining a lawyer or a doctor working at a second job in the evenings to provide for his family. But that is exactly the case with many pastors. Often the "salary" paid by the church is only a small fraction of the family's living expenses, so there is no question about Dad's taking an additional job. It's just a fact of life. Some ministers do not moonlight, but depend on their wives to work at outside jobs so that the family will be provided for.

In either case there is additional strain and tension created in the home. If the pastor is trying to work two jobs, he is constantly tired. He is also frustrated because he can't really do justice to either one. If his wife is working outside the home out of necessity, she is also in effect working two jobs. So she is constantly tired plus probably feeling guilty about things not done at home. Either way there is little time for the couple to spend together. Often their relationship suffers as a result. There are too few chances to sit down and talk things over, and little misunderstandings grow into big problems.

Other Women

Since a number of pastors' marriages are presently ending in divorce, and since the "other woman" figures prominently in many of these divorces, we are forced to consider this to be a potential problem in the ministry. Women who are not their wives, can, and do, create many problems and temptations for ministers.

There are a number of reasons for this. First of all, as we noted before, a great deal of a minister's time is spent in counseling. Much of this is marriage counseling, since divorce has become commonplace. The minister listens sympathetically to a woman's problems. This is the first time in quite a while that a man has really listened to her. Her husband and she have no real communication anymore. She misunderstands the pastor's genuine concern for her as something more.

He, on the other hand, is very flattered that this attractive woman obviously needs him. Perhaps at some point in her story she begins to cry. He can't stand to see a woman cry, so he tries to comfort her. She tells him how understanding he is. He sees how she hangs on his every word, how she really seems to appreciate him.

Besides the fact that the woman obviously desperately needs the pastor's help, he sees her when she is dressed-up and made-up for the appointment. She looks her best. She is trying to be as pleasant as possible. This is all in contrast to his wife whom he sees when she's looking good, but also when she isn't. Probably when he left her that morning she was not all dressed up. She and he also have all the hassles of everyday living together. The counselee is in a different position. She may be fighting with her husband, but with the pastor she is in the position of accepting what he tells her.

Another factor adding to the pastor's temptation is that it is a lot easier to conduct an affair without being discovered than it was a generation ago. Then most of us lived in communities where everyone knew everyone else's business. And the minister was one of the most visible people in the community. Adultery in such communities was rare. I'm sure that people were not more moral. It's just that when an affair *was* carried on, it was pretty much public information. It takes a particular kind of person to brave the certain condemnation of one's entire community, and ministers were seldom in a position to do that. There was little opportunity for clandestine affairs. Where could they go?

Today it is quite simple to drive to the next town or to another part of the city. We are not involved with more than a few neighbors, so it is quite easy to hide. Also, most of us have cars readily available to us. The mechanics of an affair are all too easy.

Besides knowing everyone else's business, the communities of yesteryear were concerned about their members. There was a communal responsibility for holding to biblical values—a responsibility to guard against crime and immorality.

The social climate has changed radically in the last couple of decades. What was unthinkable twenty years ago is now being openly practiced. Today we have been very much influenced by the individualism which is rampant in our culture. We tend to think that a neighbor's ungodly conduct is not our responsibility. Although Christians still do not condone affairs or divorce, we no longer react with the same horror. We accept and live with these things as well as with other changes in morals. Although he is not consciously thinking these things out, the minister knows that we are far past the days of wearing a scarlet letter to symbolize adultery.

Pressures

The demands put on the pastor are perhaps greater than those of any other profession. While doctors and others are also on call, it is never twenty-four hours a day, seven days a week. They have scheduled times when they are on call for a certain length of time, and then certain times off. Except for the pastor's three weeks of vacation once a year, he is always on call. And even then, if he leaves a number where he can be reached, he is often called away. We have had our vacation cut short more than once to come back because of a death in the congregation or some other emergency. Doctors are in a different situation. When they are on vacation, someone else takes care of their emergencies.

Each person who interrupts the pastor on Saturday while he is finishing his sermon preparation, or on Monday when he is supposed to be having a day off, thinks that his is the only interruption. No one stops to think that there are many, many more people with problems just as important to them, each disturbing the pastor just this once.

Lucille Lavendar writes, "It would be unfair to suggest that other occupations and professions do not have their share of stress. But . . . there are associations for doctors and lawyers, lobbyists for nearly any group, unions for trades people." She goes on to say that the presidency is probably the most high-pressure job in the world. But special pains are taken to protect the president from many of these pressures. He has a large staff to take care of many of the details for him, plus several different retreats to which he can escape via private planes. Clergymen, on the other hand, "who have all the pressures of leadership, planning, administration, writing, speaking, counseling, comforting, and diplomacy—limp along with little help and never enough time. In addition, they have to be concerned about an old car needing repair, a leaking roof, mowing the lawn, preparing income tax returns, and the drudgery of deciding which . . . bills should be paid out of a too small income."[6]

Perhaps as enervating as any of the demands that others place upon the minister are the demands he puts upon himself. A large majority of the ministers I have met are sensitive, spiritual people with a high sense of calling. They are conscious of being God's special representatives in the world. When people do not respond or things do not go well in the church, they often blame themselves. And because people expect so much from them, they try to live up to these expectations.

There are also guilt feelings because of the enormous work load. One minister wrote that he labors under a constant nagging feeling that he must be either lazy or disorganized, because he is always busy, yet never gets caught up. He says that the longer he serves a particular congregation, the more he understands the needs of his people. Then as the demands of committee meetings inside and outside the church increase, the load becomes impossible. He writes that he puts in a sixty to seventy hour week, and enjoys it, but he cannot shake the feelings of guilt from things still left undone.

In a recent article in a church paper a minister writes, "[Ministers] feel guilty when the light is on in the church, and they are at home. They feel guilty on the pulpit when they see all the people they think they should have visited. They feel guilty when they read books, and they feel guilty when they don't read. They live in guilt."[7]

I know this to be the experience of the minister with whom I live. We talk about it sometimes. Rationally, logically, it does not make sense. He knows that he works hard. He works nearly every evening as well as all day. Actually, he loves his work and would choose to do it whether or not he were being paid for it. He thrives on it. My sister-in-law says about my pastor brother, "I have come to terms with the fact that Jim will always be too busy. It's just his style." Both of these men are responding to an urgency which they feel to spread the gospel and implement its message as quickly and as well as they can. Yet the feelings of guilt persist.

Chapter 4

The Walking Wounded: Wives

The women who are married to ministers are usually also among the walking wounded. Some are nursing serious injuries; others have received only minor cuts and scrapes which seem to have healed easily without leaving any scars. Few escape completely unscathed.

Stereotype of the Minister's Wife

Pastors' wives, like their husbands, suffer from discouragement. For one thing, they and their children, like their husbands, are right up there in the public eye—on display. They are almost always introduced to others as pastors' wives. One wife reminded me that no one says, "This is Janie, our plumber's wife," or "our school-teacher's wife." But the pastor's wife is invariably presented as "our minister's wife." I had always accepted this as a compliment, knowing that my friends who introduce me this way love my husband and are proud of me. But when I thought about it I realized that it has, on occasion, put me in an uncomfortable position. No one knows quite what to say after that kind of introduction, so there is an awkward silence.

I also came to the conclusion that some of the best relationships I have with people have been begun before they realized that I was a pastor's wife. As we became better acquainted, they naturally found out. But by that time they had accepted me for myself. I am sure that some of them, particularly those who are not church members, might have been scared away at the beginning if they had known. Since the ministry is an unknown quantity to them, it often makes them more than a little uncomfortable.

The members of the congregation (and often the general public as well) tend to expect pastors' wives to be more spiritual than anyone else in the church, except for the minister himself, of course. And along with this they are expected to possess a superior Bible knowledge. This pressure can lead to deception. Several women told me that they didn't feel superspiritual, but they knew they were supposed to, so they began to fake it. It was never a deliberate decision to deceive. It just kind of happened. They simply let people believe that they fit the image that had been created for them.

In addition to these expectations about what the minister's wife is, there are expectations about what she does. These differ in amount and severity from denomination to denomination, as well as within denominations. Here is a list of some expectations which I have personally encountered: I was often expected to keep my house cleaner and in better order than anyone else; I have been expected to play the organ and/or piano for worship services and Sunday school; I was supposed to be program chairman for the Sunday school, lead the Ladies Aid, and host parties for various church groups from young people to the consistory and their wives. And of course I was required to appear at all worship services and meetings in the church or related to the church. It has also been expected that my husband and I visit all of the different families in the congregation individually.

My introduction to the stereotype of the pastor's wife came about nineteen years ago, before my husband had even entered the ministry. He was teaching school for a semester while waiting for the annual meeting of our general synod which would examine him for the ministry. The town in which he found a teaching job was small and conservative. We rented an upstairs apartment. Our landlord, a deacon in the local church, lived with his wife on the main floor of the house.

We found our landlord and his wife to be very friendly. We visited with them now and then. She would let me use her washing machine and sometimes even offered to wash the baby's diapers when she did her own wash.

All went well until, newly pregnant with my second child, I began to suffer from morning sickness. Unfortunately this nausea and general malaise was not confined to mornings. In fact, it often got progressively worse as the day wore on. This only lasted for a few weeks, but during those weeks it was hard for me to take care of a twelve-month-old toddler in addition to cooking and cleaning the apartment. Since that was the order of my priorities, the housework suffered.

Occasionally getting out of our tiny apartment took my mind off my tummy and improved my morale. One evening my husband and I got a sitter and went to the junior-senior banquet to which the teachers were also invited. The next day my landlady came knocking on my door. She proceeded to give me a dressing-down for having fluffs of dust on the stairway between the floors. Evidently she considered this stairway to be my responsibility, because the door was at the bottom. However, she and her husband also regularly used the staircase to get to two rooms which they used on our floor.

Since the conversation took place many years ago, I have forgotten most of it. But I have never forgotten her telling me that I was supposed to have my house cleaner than other people because I was a minister's wife. I was incredulous. In the first place, I had not previously come across this double standard for ministers' wives. In the second place, I wasn't one! At that point my husband was not, nor had ever been, a minister. He had simply graduated from seminary. He was not even a Bible teacher—he taught Latin and typing!

Feeling that I had somehow failed in something that was so important to her, I tried to explain that I was pregnant and not feeling well, so the dusting had not gotten done. But she was accepting no excuses. She pointed out that just the night before I had gotten dressed up and gone out to dinner. If I were feeling good enough to go out, I was not too sick to do my dusting.

When my husband came home and heard what had happened, he was more upset than I was. Although this woman was not a terrible housekeeper, her apartment was far from immaculate. My husband informed her that not only was I not a minister's wife, but I was also a very young and inexperienced wife. She, on the other hand, was much older and the wife of a deacon. So if anyone were to be an example, she should. Unfortunately, she didn't see it that way.

When we entered our first pastorate, I again ran into the set of expectations that many people hold for the minister's wife. We arrived at the end of September, having been delayed by an accident on the way in which my tailbone was broken. Since I was nearly eight months pregnant at the time, it did not heal until after the delivery. So I was having pain a great deal of the time until the baby came. I would do most of my work alternating between periods of standing up and lying down, because sitting was so painful. I carried an inflated rubber ring around with me everywhere I went, since sitting on it helped to ease the pain a bit.

Somehow, I managed to get some of the boxes unpacked, and even started toilet training my toddler. The ordination service, at which my husband was to be officially installed as pastor, was set for the end of October.

There were no draperies in the large living-dining room of the house when we arrived. It was assumed that I would do something about this. My father and mother-in-law had come to visit to attend the ordination. Mom said that she would help me make the drapes. We drove thirty-five miles to the city to buy fabric, and then both of us sewed nonstop to get them hung in time for the service. In our haste we even sewed one set together so that they could not be opened, and we had to rip them out. But we made it in time, except for the hems which were temporarily folded under.

I played the organ for the service while perched on my rubber ring. Afterwards I served sandwiches, dessert, and coffee to about thirty people in the parsonage. Everyone seemed to think it was my job, and I never questioned it. I remember having two long tables set up in that large room.

Our second baby was born on November 14. This released pressure from my tailbone, so it started healing very nicely. I was nursing the baby, and all was going well. The basement still contained boxes needing to be unpacked, many windows were waiting for curtains to be sewn, the toilet training of our toddler had hit an impasse, and I remember brief moments when I doubted that, should I live to be eighty, I would ever get my dishes and ironing all done at once, but all was well. My husband was enjoying his work, and the people couldn't have been nicer to us. We were showered with everything from eggs and chickens to cookies, honey, and cream.

Then, about the middle of December, it happened. One of the Sunday school teachers came up to me and asked me what I was doing about "the Christmas concert," referring to the Sunday school program. I had no idea what she meant. I repeated her own words back to her, stalling for time: "The Christmas concert?" Then she explained, as one might to a not very bright child, that of course the minister's wife always took care of the Christmas concert. This meant that she produced and directed it, and she usually wrote the script as well.

The previous minister's wife was an older woman with no children. She loved to do this sort of thing and had many years of experience. I, on the other hand, was a very young, very busy mother of two babies, one only a few weeks old, and I had never even taught a Sunday school class.

The really incredible part of this episode is that I did it. I really did, on two weeks' notice, throw together some sort of a program. I still remember standing up there directing with perspiration streaming down my face. Immediately afterward I went home, nursed the baby, and collapsed in bed.

They never should have asked, I shouldn't have even considered accepting, and my husband should not have allowed it. But at that time none of us knew any better.

My husband and I lived with the stereotype of the minister's wife for those four years of our first charge. But we did our best to challenge it. After my initial acquiescence, we realized that my physical and mental welfare were at stake. It was simply not humanly possible for me to fulfill the congregation's role expectations for me while also doing my job as wife and mother. It was a matter of survival.

When demands were presented to me that we felt were unreasonable, we said "no" as tactfully as possible. We also tried to encourage the capable laymen to develop their abilities so that they would not be so dependent on the minister and his wife. This, predictably, met with a great deal of resistance at first. A few of the more courageous were willing to attempt to take leadership in certain areas immediately; others balked. But by the end of our stay we felt that a measurable amount of progress had been made.

Now, I do not want to give the impression that there was constant tension between me and the congregation. I look back on those years as some of the most enjoyable in our ministry. My husband and I were both novices, so we made our share of mistakes. The congregation accepted our failures graciously. Mostly they pretended that they didn't even notice. They were continually asking my husband how I was adjusting to life on the prairie, and they followed up their words with action. Along with gifts of food went offers of help. We seldom paid a baby-sitter. There were plenty of substitute mothers in the congregation who would have been insulted if we had tried to pay them.

These dear hearts and gentle people found many of my ways to be strange, but I felt that they totally accepted me. They appreciated the fact that my husband and I were serving as their pastor and wife, and they showed their appreciation. We still make visits back there occasionally and almost have the feeling that we never left.

Besides the expectations that others have for us, we have to deal with the expectations we have for ourselves as pastors' wives. As one young wife put it, "We're as guilty as the congregation when it comes to putting the pressure on. Our image is way up there and we ourselves have put the finishing touches on it." To a large extent we too have stereotyped the minister's wife by trying to conform to our own idealistic and unrealistic mental image of what we should be.

Loneliness

Another source of discouragement for the women who are married to ministers is the loneliness that often seems to be a part of life in the parsonage. Though all pastors' wives are not agreed on this point, a majority of the women whom I talked to said that they do not have a close friend. Some said that having a really good friend in the congregation didn't seem possible. A large majority of the women did not think it would be right. They thought that singling one woman out for special friendship would be wrong because those not chosen would feel slighted.

A few told of disastrous experiences resulting from such attempts. Each of them had had a close friend in the congregation in whom she had confided for a shorter or longer period of time. In each case the friend violated the trust placed in her by telling these secrets to others in the church. Soon the whole congregation knew. The private life of the pastor's wife became public knowledge. Each of these women felt somewhat bitter about her experience. Each vowed that she would never try to have a best friend in a congregation again.

A large proportion of ministers' wives, then, have no real friends. They have many acquaintances with whom they are friendly. Perhaps they even spend a lot of time with some of these people. But there is no one with whom they can let their hair down. There is no baring of the soul—no feeling of being known, flaws and all, and still being accepted. This is an important psychic need that is being left unmet. A basic psychological tenet is that everyone needs at least one person who knows him very well, including his weaknesses, and still loves him with no strings attached.

Of course husbands and wives can and should meet this need in each other. But I believe it makes for a healthier situation when the spouse is not the only real friend a person has. For one thing, it places a tremendous burden on the marriage relationship when this is the case. This relationship then has to bear the entire responsibility for affirming each spouse's identity. So when there is a quarrel or a misunderstanding between husband and wife, it is weighed down with the added encumbrance of posing a threat to either spouse's feeling of worth as a person. If a woman's husband is the only person that is close to her who really knows her and accepts her the way she is and he is angry with her, she is in a precarious position indeed. This causes misunderstandings between husband and wife to be blown way out of proportion.

There is another reason for having a best friend in addition to one's husband. Men and women are different. We can argue about whether most of the differences between women and men are innate—given to us by our Creator—or whether they are culturally conditioned. In any case, they are there. They exist. A woman and a man, no matter how committed they are to one another, no matter how great their relationship, can never totally understand each other. And men as a group and women as a group will perhaps never truly understand each other. I am continually amazed at the naiveté of otherwise sophisticated, intelligent men where women are concerned. They seem completely oblivious to the fact of being pursued, or to being manipulated in a way that is instantly obvious to any other woman. Perhaps that is as it should be. This keeps the added dimension of mystery in any man-woman relationship. In any case, men understand men, and women understand women. And so a good friend of the same sex can be a friend in a way that a spouse cannot, no matter how good the marriage. So the lack of a best friend is keenly felt by many women in the parsonage.

Another source of unhappiness for many wives is the fact that they don't get to see their husbands enough. They do not have enough time together, either as husband and wife, or as a family. It seems that family time is seldom put into the minister's schedule. And even when it is, a telephone call can, and often will, disrupt the family time. Unexpected calls, whether in person or by telephone, so often take precedence over wife and family.

And even when the husband is with the family bodily, it is often hard for him to be completely with them mentally and emotionally. His mind may be preoccupied with someone else's problems. Or even if he is not preoccupied, the wife may have the feeling that he is making a special effort to take time with his family because he knows that he should. A frequent complaint of many of the wives with whom I talked was the feeling that they always came second. They felt that the church came first with their husbands. This leads to feelings of loneliness even when their husbands are physically present.

Money Problems

Although the situation seems to be improving in this area, money problems are still a reality for a large proportion of pastors. Lucille Lavender gives statistics from a pamphlet put out by the U.S. Department of Labor which lists occupations from the highest paid on down. "Out of 432 occupations listed, clergymen ranked 317 . . . (they) rank with the lowest-paying occupations and with unskilled labor. . . . Though they rank next to the bottom economically, educationally they rank with the top earning occupations—lawyers, physicians, dentists, judges, college professors, scientists, engineers, and managers. Most of the 107 below their earning rank did not graduate from high school, while many did not go beyond the eighth grade."[8]

The ministers' wives are the ones who must do most of the coping with the financial problems. They must make do or do without. Many of the wives I interviewed said that they sew a lot of their own and their family's clothes, and they spend a great deal of time canning and freezing food during the summer. Some also have their own vegetable gardens which they tend. Although most of them said they enjoy doing these things, they often feel that these activities take time that they can ill afford, with the press of family duties and church work. Yet they are economic necessities. If their families are going to be decently fed and clothed, they must do these things.

An added dimension to the problem is that ministers *are* professionals. Often their friends are others in the professions who are making much more money than they are. The ministers cannot afford a life-style similar to that of their friends. They cannot afford the meals out, expensive cars and other vehicles, entertaining, and clothes. When they stop to think about it, their friends realize this. And yet the pressure is there. Neither staying home nor always letting someone else pick up the check is very satisfying. As one ex-minister put it: the minister is completely surrounded by affluence in which he cannot share.

Again, this is usually harder on the wives. Perhaps it is because we have more of an appreciation for nice things. I hate to think that we women are by nature more materialistic than men. Probably it is because we are forced to spend a lot of our time working with material things. It usually falls to us to decorate the house and keep it clean, cook the food, and plan the family's wardrobes and keep them in repair. So it is part of our job to work with possessions, and it is often hard not to desire nicer ones. This is especially the case when the people all around us have things that are much nicer than ours.

Moves

The frequent moves which a pastor's family must make are another problem for many of the wives. Again, most of the trauma is the wife's to absorb. The husband simply packs up his books and begins making sermons, counseling, etc., in the new setting. Of course he must learn many new names and faces; but his wife is expected to do that as well as he. In addition, she usually must take care of unpacking and putting away all of the family's household effects, find the children's new schools, and try to ferret out an acceptable doctor, dentist, baby-sitter, piano teacher, dry cleaner, and shoe repairman. These are not easy tasks, as anyone who has recently moved a family knows.

There are, of course, others who make frequent moves, such as construction workers and junior executives. However, most professional people make a choice early in their careers and stay in the same location from then on. Even the junior executives usually make only a couple of moves before they settle more or less permanently. But the norm for ministers is still to move every few years. One woman whom I interviewed said that she had moved twenty-five times!

There are some notable exceptions to this pattern. Some well-known ministers make a career out of one congregation. But these are still unusual cases. Most pastors are not able to do that.

A minister friend and I were talking about this one day. We were discussing the length of time it takes for a pastor to become established in a community so that people know him and trust him. He can then really begin to be effective. My friend and I agreed that the minimum time required for this is two or three years. But many ministers move after three or four years. What a waste! My friend went on to say that no doctor decides after a few years that he needs new patients—that his "work is finished" in that community. Neither do teachers or lawyers feel a pressure to leave a place after a few years (or worse yet, get transferred!). Why do we assume that a minister must leave after a few years?

This system is hard on the minister and his children. But his wife is affected the most of all. Besides having to deal with the mechanics of the move—with all the hundreds of details to be taken care of—she must act as a shock absorber for the others. She will be helping her husband and children to adjust to the new situation, smoothing the way for them. Studies on tension and trauma show that a move is a significant stress-producer. The move of a minister's family involves a change in church activities, social activities, and work conditions as well as a change of residence. This ranks it very high on the stress scale. The only events which have a higher impact are the death of a spouse, a divorce, or a jail term.

The Parsonage

Living in a parsonage is one aspect of the ministerial life which appears to be in a state of transition. Many of the pastors and wives whom I interviewed still lived in parsonages, and a few had been in their own homes for a number of years. But a surprisingly large number had lived in parsonages previously and were now home-owners, or were going through the process of leaving parsonages for their own homes. It appears that many denominations are re-thinking the whole idea of a parsonage. They realize that it may be very unfair to send their pastors off into retirement with no equity built up in a house. The recent incredible rise in the price of real estate has brought this problem sharply into focus. Because of this, many congregations have sold their parsonages and now give their pastors a housing allowance instead. This way they are free to buy a house or to rent, whichever they prefer.

We have lived in parsonages throughout our ministry, and I have personally felt, up until now, that the advantages outweighed the disadvantages. Each time that we moved I had a small baby, and I found it convenient to have a house ready for us to move into. With the exception of a rented house which we were in for a year, the parsonages we have lived in have all been up-to-date and comfortable. While we were packing to move out of that rented house, we had to let prospective buyers come through to look at it. They did not come at convenient times, and they tracked mud and slush on my carpet. I then appreciated not having the trauma of selling a house added to the other tensions of a move.

But from my reading and from talking to ministers and wives, I realize that my generally happy experience with parsonages is not the norm. And a great many, perhaps most, ministers' families must still live in houses provided for them by the congregation.

One of the difficulties seems to be in letting the parsonage be the minister's home. Since the house belongs to the church, there is a tendency for people of the congregation to feel that they have a claim on it. They often think that it should be available for meetings whenever they decide or, at the very least, whenever additional space is needed.

Some wives have even reported to me that many of the members of the congregation think that they can come over to the parsonage whenever they please, because after all it belongs to them. This problem seems to be most acute in the cases where the furnishings of the house are a part of the parsonage and do not belong to the pastor. Evidently when they are furnishing the house, some of these parishioners do not give the furniture with no strings attached. They still feel that the things are partly theirs.

There is a related problem experienced by those living in parsonages when the house is next door to the church. Whenever something is going on at church, people tend to run next door for something or other. They need a key for something, or the telephone at church is being used, so they ask to use the parsonage phone. Whenever they are making a meal or serving food, they run out of something and have to borrow it from the parsonage.

Daily Vacation Bible School can mean people in and out of the parsonage nonstop. Even when the pastor's wife is not teaching a class, she finds that it takes a great deal of her time just answering the door. Sometimes she doesn't even get to answer the door. Last summer as I was dressing for the Bible school program and was standing in my slip, I found myself eyeball to eyeball with a young boy whom I had never seen before. He was one of the Bible school children waiting for the program to begin, and he had simply walked in my back door. He than ran out giggling and began to tell his friends that he had seen me in my underwear!

In some of the reading I have done, I have come across some real horror stories about parsonages. If the writers were not Christians whom I trusted, I would hardly be able to believe some of them. There were tales of woodstoves, of plumbing which seldom worked, of hauling water to do the washing, and of old, drafty houses which were impossible to heat or clean. I certainly hope that these houses are no longer serving as parsonages.

None of the women whom I interviewed complained that their houses were lacking in such fundamentals as decent furnaces or hot water. But they did talk about committees which were not always helpful when things would break down. Some told of painting and wallpapering that had been promised when they moved in, and a year or two later it was still not done.

Many mentioned the fact that churches do not make good landlords. They felt that if they were renting, the landlord would have to see to it that the house was kept in good repair. A church committee, on the other hand, is often lax. And since the minister and his wife don't want to make trouble, they live with varying degrees of inconvenience. Sometimes they are seriously inconvenienced.

There is also the obvious problem that no one house is going to fit every family's needs perfectly. What seems just right for the family with five children seems to the childless couple like far too many rooms. Even worse is the too-small house trying to accommodate a growing family.

And then there's the furniture. If the minister and his wife buy enough furniture for a large house, they may have nowhere to put a lot of it after the next move when the house doesn't include a family room and an extra bedroom.

Color can pose another problem. Since the carpet and drapes are usually already in each house, the family's furniture has to go with it somehow, whether the colors are complementary or not. Many pastors' wives have told me that they feel they have to buy furniture in basic tones when they would like, say, a bright red sofa. But even if the sofa would fit in the present house, it might be a disaster in the next. So a safe beige is bought instead. Living all their lives with basic colors is no problem for some wives. But others feel this to be very constricting. One woman told me that her main reason for wanting her own home was to get some color into it. Her artistic nature had been stifled for so many years. Now she felt that she could finally express her individuality in her home.

The Phone

A constant interruption in the lives of most ministers' wives is the telephone. Besides the normal calls which any woman receives, the pastor's wife must take a large number of calls for her husband. If he is not at the church, people call his house for him. If he is not there (which is usually the case), the caller will often ask his question of the wife. As likely as not she has no idea what the problem is about, but she has to listen anyway, even though she cannot help.

There also seem to be a number of people in every congregation who *always* call the parsonage first when looking for the pastor. In spite of the fact that his study is at church, they seem to have the idea that he spends his time hanging around the house. When they are told that he's at the church, they act surprised. And the next time they call the house again.

I have been late for appointments on many occasions because of phone calls at the last minute. I often think that I should take the phone off the hook while I am preparing to leave, and quickly put it back before I go out the door. But I never do.

One pastor's wife, realizing that her housework and other obligations were suffering, began to keep track of the time spent on telephone calls for her husband. She found that in one two-week period she had spent an average of three hours a day taking calls and listening to people who really wanted to talk to her husband! There were fifteen calls one morning while she was trying to mop and wax the kitchen floor. Little wonder that pastors' wives become discouraged.

Chapter 5

The Walking Wounded: Children

In addition to ministers and their wives, their children are often included in the ranks of the walking wounded. In my interviews with pastors and their wives we discussed their children and the effects living in the parsonage had had upon them. A number of these ministers and their wives had themselves been "preachers' kids," so they were able to give me the benefit of their experience both from the perspective of a child and that of a parent.

The majority of the people I interviewed indicated that although there were a few minor problems—mostly unfair expectations—their children were managing to cope pretty well. They didn't think that being in the parsonage was particularly traumatic for their children.

However, I did hear of a few truly dreadful experiences of ministers' children. One woman told me, while trying hard to keep from weeping, that her children have had to take a lot of abuse because of their position. She told of teachers who had mentioned in class that her children should know all the answers because they were "preachers' kids." She also related an incident in which one of her children had been running in the church building with several others, including the son of the Christian Education committee chairman. While completely ignoring her own unruly child, the chairman had grabbed the minister's son and told him that ministers' kids shouldn't act that way.

When he was in high school, this same child was subjected to repeated taunts from his classmates. They kept telling him that his dad was a lousy preacher, and sometimes they would hit him. Once his nose was broken in the hall by a boy who said that he wished the preacher and his family would get out of town. He was also called a "fairy" because he was musical and he wore his hair a little different from the others. His mother said that he had had terrible social problems because his father was a minister.

One of the most poignant stories I heard concerned a young preacher's son who started experimenting with drugs when he was in college. When he was in medical school he took an overdose. He did not die, but the effects were terrible. At the time that I saw his mother, he wasn't able to talk. They were beginning speech therapy but were not at all certain that it would be successful. His motor control was very bad—it took him a couple of hours just to shave and dress himself. The doctors were not hopeful that the situation would improve very much, if at all.

His mother didn't blame his problem with drugs on the fact that he was a minister's son. She thinks he probably would have tried them in any case. But she did think that his position complicated things and kept him from getting help. Because he knew that his parents and everyone in the church would strongly disapprove of his actions, he took exquisite care to keep his habit hidden. He indicated to his sister that his guilt over his misuse of his body was terrible, so it drove him into a deeper involvement. He didn't dare let anyone know what he was doing. His abuse of drugs was his own terrible secret until finally his sister suspected what was going on. Even then he tried to swear her to secrecy. His sister immediately alerted his parents, but they were not able to reach him in time to avert the tragedy.

In another interview, an ex-minister's wife related that all three of her sons very deeply involved in the drug culture for several years. They were all dealers, operating out of her home. She never found out what was going on until much later, although she knew that they were hanging around with a bad crowd and were not paying much attention to their schoolwork. Although all three were very bright and had previously been good students, they finally dropped out of school. Their mother said that their parents' divorce was a dramatic turning point in their lives. They had been normal, well-adjusted children, doing better-than-average work in school. Suddenly they seemed to have no interest in studying, sports or music—all of which had been important to them before. The middle boy, particularly, was very bitter toward his father. He said over and over that he didn't see how a minister could leave his wife for another woman. The son became very cynical about religion, figuratively shaking his fist at God. He had always idolized his father because he was a "man of God." When he so suddenly revealed his feet of clay, the son couldn't handle the situation. It took six years before he was able to speak to his father and begin a reconciliation.

Double Standard for PK's

Though not as life-shattering as the experiences we've just noted, a number of specific problems that seem to belong uniquely to ministers' children were mentioned by parents. The one that I encountered the most was mentioned earlier—unfair expectations. There seems to be a double standard operating here. Over and over I heard, "They are expected to be better than other kids" or "The teachers expect them to know all the answers." If any young people are ever asked to volunteer their services in any way, the pastor's child will be first on the list of those to be called.

It isn't only adults that put this kind of pressure on them, either. Their own peers are evidently just as guilty, particularly their peers within the church community. One of our daughters used to complain that they would never start the youth group meeting until she was there, even though she wasn't an officer. She resented the fact that although she was usually on time, everyone noticed the times she wasn't. When others were late it didn't seem to matter, but when she wasn't quite on time it was a big deal. Friends of ministers' kids, as well as adults, tend to think they should behave better, take more responsibility, and be—if not more spiritual—at least more knowledgeable about spiritual matters than other children.

Unfortunately even the ministers and wives themselves often put undue pressure on their children. They themselves are under pressure to perform, to be superspiritual, to give leadership, etc., and they pass these same pressures onto their children by extension. They consider their families to be part of themselves, so, sometimes consciously, sometimes unconsciously, they demand that their children measure up to the same standard that they are trying to meet. Sometimes these standards are fair and good; perhaps as often they are not. One mother said, "You want to please the congregation. Since you think that they expect your children to perform in a certain way, you put pressure on them to do so, often without realizing it." As another mother put it, "There have been times

when the kids had a bit of the feeling that their folks were more concerned about their image than they were about them."

Negative Expectations

In certain communities or in certain congregations the minister's children may be in a kind of double bind. On the one hand,
they're expected to act somewhat better than other children; on the
other hand, there is also the often widely believed myth that
preachers' kids tend to be unruly, hard to handle, and rebellious.
Within the framework of this mind-set, any time a minister's child
fails in any way, those labels are applied to him. It's a kind of
"heads you win, tails I lose" situation.

Another difficulty that was mentioned a number of times by
both pastors and wives was the tendency to put the ministry ahead
of their families. They felt that their children often got what was left
of their time and energy. Sometimes the children's emotional needs
went unmet while Daddy and Mommy were busy ministering to
other people.

Lack of privacy was another closely related problem. Some of
the people whom I talked to mentioned that their children had a
hard time accepting people coming and going in the parsonage at
all hours, often unannounced. Several times it was mentioned that
not only would people not call ahead of time when they were coming, but they wouldn't even knock before entering the house. This
was mentioned more frequently by those pastors and wives living in
parsonages than by those living in houses which they owned themselves. The most problems in this area seemed to occur in the situations in which not only the parsonage belonged to the congregation,
but the furniture in it as well. One ex-pastor's wife told me that she
always enjoyed having people in the house, but her children resented it more and more as they got older. They felt that they
weren't really free to be themselves because there was always someone besides the family around. They wanted people to respect their
privacy.

A few of the wives I talked to mentioned the effect that gossip
about their husbands has on the children. When someone starts a
rumor about the pastor, the kids don't know how to react. And
then if there is serious trouble in the congregation, it can have a
devastating effect on a child.

One minister's wife who grew up in a parsonage told of the pain and trauma that she suffered as a child because of such a situation. When she was a teenager, there was a big blow-up in the church. It became quite public. People took sides, and her dad was in the middle of it all. One of the things that especially puzzled and hurt her was the fact that some of the people who were the most vocal in tearing her father down were people who had previously been his friends and staunchest supporters.

After that experience she learned to keep herself in reserve. She held people at arm's length. She refused to really get close to anyone for fear of being hurt the way her father had been. As a minister's wife, this became a real problem for her. It took her a long time to work it through in dialogue with herself and with God. She wanted to have a ministry—to let the Lord use her in peoples' lives—but she was afraid. She held back. She finally accepted the fact that in order to minister to people, one must be vulnerable. She has now learned to give of herself. She realizes that God has given her the abilities she needs to reach out to people and that He will protect her.

Chapter 6

What Is Marriage?

In order to find some answers to the problems facing marriage in the parsonage today, we will have to begin by looking at marriage itself. What is God's idea of marriage? What should a Christian marriage be? These are questions that need to be asked and answered by ministers and their wives as well as by anyone else. Their marriages are not exemplary relationships by definition—simply because the partners are in special kingdom service. Pastors and their wives do not have any special revelation or guidance on running a marriage. On the contrary, their relationships are sustaining special stresses and tensions, as we have seen. Furthermore, they may be afraid to openly admit these situations, since people expect so much from their marriages.

Obviously thorough coverage of all aspects of marriage in one chapter is impossible. But since through a basic definition and framework of marriage we can better discuss solutions to the problems that face pastors and their wives, we will briefly review some of the important elements of living together successfully.

Marriage Is Work

One aspect of marriage that we might as well face from the beginning is that of work—hard work, continuous work. We must work when we feel like it and work when we don't feel like it—particularily when we don't feel like it. Marriages are not made in heaven in the sense that wedded bliss drops down from the sky ready-made after a couple says the "I do's." Even when they are Christians and have taken their vows in front of God and His people, there is no such thing as living happily ever after without a great deal of effort.

The first thing that working at marriage means is time. Time must be scheduled by both partners for planning, for setting priorities, and then for working out the plans. Each husband and wife must sit down together and work through such questions as: What does God require from us as marriage partners? What do we expect from each other and ourselves? Where do we want to be in a year, in five years, in thirty years? How are we going to handle our money? Who is going to do which household chores? How are we going to raise the children God may give us?

Communication between marriage partners is not a one-time thing. It is not a little talk that a couple has in which these problems are permanently solved—decisions made once and for all and put on file somewhere. Communication is an ongoing thing. We must work at it all of our married lives. We must talk, keep talking, and then talk some more. There is no such thing as overcommunication.

Someone has said that a good rule of thumb is to assume that your partner has no idea of what you are thinking or feeling, and proceed from there. This is an excellent piece of advice. It is so easy to assume too much, and then wonder why we aren't understood.

Marriage is a lifetime of studying each other's needs and then doing our best to fill them. One person can never meet all the needs of another, of course. Nor should he. The best marriages are those in which each person has his or her own resources. Marriage should never be an escape from singleness. If a person is not capable of living a productive single life, he is not going to make a very good marriage partner either.

Nevertheless, one of the great joys of marriage is having someone who knows what our own intensely personal needs are and tries to meet them. This does indeed require work from my husband. I am, among other things, a complex bundle of contradictions. I am very capable in certain areas, and seem to have the intelligence of a five-year-old in others. I have always made high scores in tests involving reasoning skills, and I am a natural speller. But mechanically I am a total loss. I even have a terrible time working the latch on any screen door. If all the world had my brand of intelligence, we would still be hunting with bows and arrows and cooking over open fires. We wouldn't even have books to read, because no one would know how to print them.

I also am completely devoid of any rudiments of a sense of direction. Even though we have lived here for ten years, whenever there is a detour of a few blocks, I become hopelessly lost. Sometimes someone will say that his sense of direction becomes confused in a strange place. It's all the same to me. A strange place or home—I must use maps in both. I have gotten to the point where I can find a number of places without a map. But I often cannot get from one of these places to another without coming home in between.

My husband has learned to meet these needs of mine. He has drawn more maps for me than he would be able to count. He will also run errands for me if it would be difficult for me to find my way; or he will accompany me even when it is not particularly convenient for him. I know that I can depend on him for these things.

There are some needs which my husband has which might seem equally silly. I am trying to meet these needs for him as well. For instance, grocery stores completely baffle him. He unfailingly brings home the wrong thing, even when I give him a very complete description of the item. He does only a little better in department stores. So I do all of our shopping, including buying his clothes. I only bring him along when he must have a suit fitted. I even buy his shoes by myself, only occasionally exchanging a pair when the fit is not right.

He also has a terrible time finding things. He can't find the pliers in his tool drawer, or the aspirin in the medicine cabinet. I can say, "It's on the left side of the middle shelf." There will be a pause and then, "I don't see it." So I come, and there it is, on the left side of the middle shelf. I never will understand how he can't see it. But then, it's hard for him to understand that I can't find my way around.

Each person has his own idiosyncrasies—his own special areas in which he needs extra attention. No one is all of a piece. People who are very strong personalities are nevertheless vulnerable in certain areas. Bright, capable, assertive people cry too.

As we grow and develop, our needs are constantly changing. We outgrow some of our little hangups as we mature. Unfortunately, we may acquire a few new ones along the way. Or a tragedy or other circumstances in our lives create a whole new set of needs. So each marriage partner must always be sensitive to these needs. This is indeed work. And it is constant—it cannot be worked in at times when it may be convenient.

Working at marriage demands emotional energy. A partnership cannot survive on leftover bits of time here and there after our best has been given to everything else. We must find time for each other—block it off on our calendars if necessary—when we are at our physical and mental best. It is easy to slide into the habit of giving everyone else our best and neglecting our good manners and courtesies at home. Husbands and wives deserve the best from each other.

Marriage Is Play

Marriage is work, but it is also play. We know this when we first get married. At least we all expect our honeymoons to be fun. But often when we return to our everyday routines we forget to play together.

An encouraging percentage of the ministers and wives I talked to said that they regularly took time off for dates with their spouses. Sometimes these were dates for dinner at elegant restaurants; often they were just for coffee and dessert. One wife said that every Monday, without fail, she and her husband pack a picnic supper in the car and drive to some secluded spot to eat it together. They do this all year long, regardless of the weather. They live in a part of the country where the weather is suitable for picnicking most of the year. In really bad weather they eat their meal in the back of the station wagon. Another wife said that her husband and she ate at a restaurant once a week and usually also went to a play, a concert, or a movie afterwards.

One man told me that he and his wife went for a very special weekend four times a year—once every three months. They really pamper themselves in these few days. They go to a nice motel, sleep in, and go out for all meals. They often read books on marriage together during this time. Occasionally they do some window-shopping or sight-seeing. They budget nearly a week's pay each time for this outing. They leave Sunday evening after the second church service, and come back on Tuesday evening.

My husband and I go out to dinner together occasionally. More often we take some time at the end of an evening, after he has made a call or two, to go to a nearby restaurant for coffee and their special dessert—mud pie. (For those who may not have encountered this concoction, it is a scrumptious layering of chocolate cookie crust, coffee ice cream, fudge sauce, and whipped cream.) We sit and have a leisurely conversation while the waiter refills our coffee cups. For a couple of dollars we get the same atmosphere as if we were having dinner, but this way we can afford to do it more often. Sometimes we get as dressed up as we would for a very festive occasion. I pile my hair on top of my head, put on special eye make-up and jewelry. This helps to make us feel as if we are really out on a date.

Sex Is Fun

Sex is another part of marriage which is play. In a time when books and manuals on sexual expertise abound and all possible sexual techniques are analyzed and seriously discussed, we can lose sight of the fact that sex is fun. Larry Christenson says that in his opinion sex is one of the best ideas God ever had. I think he's right.

In fact, sex has helped me in my understanding of God. Looking down into the Grand Canyon gives me an idea of the majesty and awesomeness of God. But thinking about how He made us sexual beings makes me feel much closer to Him. It helps me to grasp the fact that He really understands me where I live. And furthermore, it shows me that He wants me to have fun. It proves that He has a sense of humor. As C. S. Lewis has said, the fact that we have bodies is the oldest joke of all. If we can keep that in mind, we will not take sex more seriously than we should.

However, the sexual side of marriage is important. To ignore its importance is to ask for trouble. Our sexual needs are very real, and as husbands and wives we must meet them for each other. One ex-minister who was forced to leave the ministry because of his extramarital affairs told me of his wife's repugnance for sex. She thought that it was an activity not really suited to people in the ministry. She saw herself and her husband as superior spiritual beings who should be above that sort of thing. She was always a very unwilling participant. When their marriage broke up, people were bewildered. She seemed such a perfect minister's wife. "But I didn't want a *minister's* wife," the man lamented. "I wanted a wife." This woman paid a terrible price for ignoring the importance of sex in marriage.

Only a generation or so ago couples were pretty much left to their own devices as far as sex was concerned. It was just assumed that after marriage sex more or less took care of itself. Today most couples realize that a good sexual relationship is not automatic. It is not a guarantee which comes with the wedding vows.

Sexual intimacy requires time and communication. Or maybe to put it better, it requires communication over a period of time. This means talking. There is often no way our partners will know what pleases us or what turns us off, without being told. There are, of course, nonverbal ways of communicating during love-making. These will also be used. But we must not be afraid of talking to each other in order to realize our full sexual potential. This talking about love-making can also go on at other opportune times during the day.

There is no point in a marriage at which it is too late to begin communicating about sex. Wherever you are in your marriage, if you have not talked about your needs and desires, now is the time to begin. All relationships have a need at different times for new beginnings. Marriage is, among other things, a number of decisions: a series of commitments. The present moment might be the best time to make a new start in this area of communication.

Marriage Means Submission

Today when anyone mentions the word "submission" a red flag goes up in a lot of minds. The idea of being a submissive wife is not popular today. We have all had our consciousness raised. We want to be free to do our own thing and submission sounds far too restrictive to us.

However, a big part of the problem is a misunderstanding of the biblical idea of submission. The Bible never talks about male domination. That is a term that our culture has invented. And probably it describes the way some husbands treat their wives. But that is a far cry from the bliblical idea of marriage.

Another problem is that some Christians have promoted a stereotype of the submissive wife—a kind of mindless doll who says, "Yes, dear—whatever you say, dear" to her husband, no matter what he might ask.

What then does the Bible have to say about what it means to be a wife? Ephesians 5:22-24 reads, "Wives, submit yourselves unto your own husbands, as unto the Lord. For the husband is the head of the wife, even as Christ is the head of the church: and he is the saviour of the body. Therefore as the church is subject unto Christ, so let the wives be to their own husbands in everything." [9] Just as the church is strongest and most effective when it is most perfectly doing the will of Christ, so we as wives will be bigger persons by submitting to our husbands.

Although as wives our destinies are bound up with our husbands, we must quickly state that this does not mean that we wives are second-class citizens. Nowhere does the Bible state or even imply that women are intrinsically inferior to men. The difference is one of role and function, not of worth or status.

This is an important distinction. Submission does not imply inferiority. Christ was submissive to the will of the Father, all the way to the cross. Yet He remained equal with the Father. His submission did not give Him reduced status or worth. On the contrary, it was exactly through His submission that His life and death gained inestimable worth.

What does submission mean in practical terms for a modern wife? It means that if there is a disagreement between husband and wife which cannot be solved by talking it out, in the end the husband must make the decision and take the responsibility for it. And the wife must accept this decision. The buck has to stop somewhere, and God has decided that it is to stop with the husband. Actually, in any relationship of equals someone has to make the final decision when there is a disagreement. Whether in social relationships or in business, there is always someone who makes the tough decisions. Sometimes there is formal agreement about who this person will be. Businesses usually designate one person as president. Often one of the group members just finds himself in the position of leader. In any case, someone becomes responsible for seeing that the right decisions are made. If this does not happen, the partnership, friendship, or business association dissolves. To protect marriage, God established the husband as the tie-breaker.

Submission is not only a passive thing, a giving-in. Incidents in which the wife gives in will be rather rare in a Christian marriage in which both partners are trying to find God's will for their lives. (Most decisions will be arrived at by consensus. Often each partner gives a bit.) Most important of all, submission is active and positive. When you submit something to a person, you put it at his disposal.

Paul says in Romans 12:1, "I beseech you therefore, brethren, by the mercies of God, that ye present your bodies a living sacrifice, holy, acceptable unto God, which is your reasonable service." In chapter 6:13 he says, "Yield yourselves . . . and your members as instruments of righteousness unto God." [10] In these passages Paul is explaining what submitting to God means. It does not mean giving Him blind, unthinking obedience. God does not want robots. If He did, He would not have created us with wills of our own. He wants our talents and abilities. But He also very much wants our intelligence.

Submission to God is the model for the wife's submission to her husband. She is to offer him all of her perhaps considerable intelligence and wisdom in the decision-making process. If she does not talk, discuss, and sometimes even argue with her husband when she has good ideas to offer, she is not being submissive. She is failing in part of her responsibility as a wife. Besides her intellect, she must offer her emotional and spiritual resources. If a wife has an insight into a particular issue and the husband chooses to ignore or reject it, it's his problem. He then takes full responsibility for the decision.

Marriage Means Headship

The husband's job as head is equally as demanding as the wife's role in submitting. The responsibility that is placed on him is nothing to be taken lightly. Continuing on in Ephesians 5, verse 25 reads, "Husbands, love your wives, even as Christ also loved the church and gave himself for it." [11] This is indeed a tall order! It means that husbands must love with a sacrificial love. They are called to subjugate their own wishes for the sake of their wives' welfare. Certainly this passage would allow no thought of a husband arbitrarily imposing his own will upon his wife. He must get his ego out of the way in making decisions. No male chauvinism permitted here.

Because they have the responsibility of leadership, God holds husbands responsible for their wives' behavior. This was made apparent as far back as the Garden of Eden. Eve took the fruit and ate it, making the decision for the family without consulting her husband. Adam flunked the test of leadership by going along with his wife's decision, even though it was clearly wrong. And yet after it was all over, God confronted Adam—addressing him as head of the family—and called him to account for what he had done. The fact that Eve had acted first, without consulting Adam, did not absolve him of responsibility.

Ever since, women have been eager to take things into their own hands, and men have often been all too willing to let them. It is easy to see why a great many men abdicate the responsibility for leadership in marriage when they are challenged by their wives. Leadership is not easy. It means taking risks and charting new paths. A leader is, by definition, out in front where he can easily be seen. He becomes vulnerable. There are always some who will take pot shots at him. It is much more comfortable to stay behind the ranks.

As head of the family, the husband is responsible for the direction in which the family moves. He must take responsibility for setting priorities and seeing that they are established. Of course in this area, too, he will welcome his wife's imput. She is as likely as he to have good ideas. Perhaps they will brainstorm together and then decide on a path to be taken.

One of the chief difficulties in understanding the biblical concept of husband-wife relationships is the Christian community's unthinking acceptance of the secular definition of head. By head the secularist means power, domination, and authority. By contrast the Bible means taking responsibility, giving of self, and serving. Jesus makes it abundantly clear what the Bible means by head when He corrects His disciples in Matthew 20:20-28. The mother of James and John came to Jesus to ask for high positions in His kingdom for her sons. Jesus told her and His disciples that the world's concept is that "great men exercise authority . . . [but] it shall not be so among you; [instead] whoever would be great among you must be your servant . . . even as the Son of Man came not to be served but to serve, and to give his life as a ransom for many."

Marriage Is Partnership

The first word we get from the Bible on man and woman is in Genesis 1:26, 27. "God said, Let us make man in our image . . . and let them have dominion over . . . all the earth . . . in the image of God created he him: male and female created he them." Man alone does not completely reflect the image of God, nor does woman alone. Together—complementing each other, making each other complete—man and woman are the crown of God's creation.

Man and woman need each other—not only in marriage, but also outside of it. We need each other intellectually, emotionally, and spiritually as well as physically. Single men need the company of women, and single women need men with whom they can interact.

But marriage is the best expression of man and woman together mirroring God. The second chapter of Genesis tells us that woman was made from man and for man. But the reason given for her existence is that man was incomplete without her. He needed her for wholeness. Husbands and wives are equally dependent on one another.

We mentioned before that in a Christian marriage in which the husband takes his role as head of the family seriously and the wife understands what it is to submit, most decisions are arrived at by consensus. When an important decision must be made which involves his wife, the husband will try to get as much input as possible from her. Probably the two of them will set aside a time to discuss the issue together. Each of them will submit his ideas and also let his feelings on the matter be known. If an issue is emotionally charged for one of them, they will try to understand why this is so. Emotions, as well as ideas, must be faced and dealt with.

Husbands and wives share equally in the kingdom. First Peter 3:7 says that they are "heirs together of the grace of life." [12] They are equal partners in marriage, each with a specific task to perform. Since together they reflect the image of God, they will grow best—intellectually, emotionally, and spiritually—if they grow together. Together they will develop their potential to its fullest.

This means studying the Bible together, sharing together spiritually. It also means sharing ideas and emotions. Many husbands and wives find that an excellent way to grow together intellectually is to read a number of the same books and then discuss them together. My husband and I have always done this. He will get all excited about a book and bring it home for me to read so that we can talk about it and perhaps find implications for our lives and for our ministry. We are each always watching for articles and books which will be of interest to the other. I look for illustrations and other material which might be useful for sermon-making or counseling. He keeps a lookout for anything that would be helpful in my writing and speaking. Actually, part of our work is done together, and for the rest we're pretty much dealing with the same subject matter. We are always involved in thinking issues through together.

The Bible always talks in terms of fellowship, of community. And the family is the primary community. The idea that a man and wife should go off in different directions—each doing his own thing to find maturity and fulfillment—is not biblical. This kind of thinking is a product of the culture around us which is very individualistic. Individualism is *not* a biblical idea. It is true that each person is responsible to God for his own commitment to Christ and for his own actions. But from the beginning of biblical history salvation came through families. When God called Abraham out He called him with his family and told him that he would be a blessing to all the *families* of the earth—not all the individuals. The whole Israelite nation was nothing more than an extended family. The Bethel Series, a comprehensive Bible study which many churches have been using, shows so clearly how God works with families all the way from Abraham through the New Testament.

The prophets told Israel about Pentecost, saying that their sons and daughters would prophesy, and then Peter told them again in his sermon on Pentecost that the promise was to them and their children. That same day the Holy Spirit came on the group as they were meeting. He didn't come to isolated believers in different places. And Jesus revealed himself after His resurrection to the group of believers. The Holy Spirit always does his best work in a group. That's why the fellowship of Christians is so important to us. It's also the reason that retreats and other special meetings are so effective. The impact is multiplied because we build each other up; we need each other. That's the way God meant it to be. And it's the same thing in marriage.

Marriage Is Commitment

Marriage is commitment. These are words that need to be burned into our very souls today. We are all familiar with the words contained in most wedding forms, "For this reason a man shall leave his father and mother and be joined to his wife, and the two shall become as one flesh." But are we really conscious of the fact that this was God's commentary on man at creation (Gen. 2:24) and that Jesus strongly reaffirmed these words to the Pharisees? In Matthew 19:4-6 He chides them for not knowing God's words on the subject. Then He authoritatively and unequivocally adds the well-known phrase, "What therefore God has joined together, let not man put asunder." Maybe this phrase is so familiar that we no longer listen to what it says or realize who is speaking it. Perhaps it has become so much a part of the ritual we take for granted that we forget that its introduction must be a resounding "Thus saith the Lord!"

Marriage is built on love. Couples who marry are usually in love. That is, they are physically attracted to each other and desire each other's company. They experience excitement when they are together and generally feel good about each other. It would probably not be wise, in our culture, for a couple to marry without this kind of love being present.

But this being in love, this feeling we have for each other, is not the essence of love. Love is an act of the will. The classic chapter on love is 1 Corinthians 13, where Paul defines love for us. He gives us God's description of love. Verses 4, 5 read, "Love is very patient and kind, never jealous or envious, never boastful or proud, never haughty or selfish or rude. Love does not demand its own way. It is not irritable or touchy. It does not hold grudges and will hardly even notice when others do it wrong." Then come the powerful seventh and eighth verses, "If you love someone you will be loyal to him no matter what the cost. You will always believe in him, always expect the best of him, always stand your ground in defending him . . . love goes on forever." [13]

There's no provision here for the idea that "we're just not in love anymore." Love is *not* a feeling, although good feelings usually accompany love. Love is a decision—a decision to hang in there, even when the going gets rough. *Especially* when the going gets rough. This is what 1 Corinthians 13 is talking about. There would be no call to "stand your ground in defending him" if there were not the assumption that at some time or another he was going to need defense. The King James Version says that love "endureth all things," which gives the same thought. Love is not all moonlight and roses. Much of the time there will be a lot to simply be endured.

In fact, love doesn't really come into its own until it has done some suffering. Any parent knows that. And yet a father or mother who would never think of disowning his child because the going gets a bit rough will seriously consider divorce because of problems facing the marriage. The word from the Lord is: endure. Romans 5:3-5 reads, "We can rejoice, too, when we run into problems and trials, for we know that they are good for us—they help us learn to be patient. And patience develops strength of character in us and helps us trust God more each time we use it until finally our hope and faith are strong and steady. Then, when that happens, we are able to hold our heads high no matter what happens and know that all is well, for we know how dearly God loves us, and we feel this warm love everywhere within us because God has given us the Holy Spirit to fill our hearts with his love." [14]

Chapter 7

Words to Seminarians and Pre-Sems

After having talked to hundreds of pastors and wives, I am still optimistic about the ministry and ministerial marriages; no situation is hopeless when compared with God's abundant grace and power. He can redeem any life, any marriage. And yet, there is no sense in starting marriage with unnecessary difficulties. A great deal of heartbreak and misery can be avoided by the careful choice of a wife. Prevention is still the best cure.

Love Is a Decision

Someone may say, however, "But you don't advertise for a wife, or go shopping for one. You just meet someone, fall in love, and get married." Admittedly, one does not set out to find a wife the way he would look for a car to buy. But surely as much care should be taken in the selection of a life's partner as in the choice of a car. And yet a person who would never choose a car which is impractical or far too expensive simply because he "fell in love with it" will often choose a wife who is not right for him. And he will give that very reason—he fell in love with her—as if there were nothing he could do about it.

As mentioned previously, love is a decision—a commitment. It is not just a feeling. And it certainly is not something that just happens to us, outside of our control. True love is a deliberate choice. Although even simply letting it happen is also a choice. Even simply deciding to be passive is as much a choice as deciding to act.

Date Only Christians

It all begins with dating. The first rule is to date only Christians. That seems obvious. Dating leads to marriage, and since you cannot have a non-Christian wife, you don't date non-Christian girls. The Bible leaves no room for doubt about the possibility of marrying a non-Christian. Second Corinthians 6:14-17 reads: "Do not be mismated with unbelievers. For what partnership have righteousness and iniquity? Or what fellowship has light with darkness? . . . Or what has a believer in common with an unbeliever? . . . For we are the temple of the living God; as God said, . . . I will be their God, and they shall be my people. Therefore come out from among them and be separate from them, says the Lord."

But every so often a man rationalizes that he will be able to convert this beautiful, talented, non-Christian girl, and then she will make a wonderful wife. Or a young woman thinks that her wonderful boyfriend will become a Christian after they get serious about each other. They seem so right for each other in so many ways. And isn't it commendable to lead someone to the Lord?

Generally speaking, it never works. We have seen this sad story acted out many, many times in our ministry. When a fellow becomes serious about a girl even though she is not a Christian, it doesn't take long before that girl realizes she is more important to him than Christ is. Obviously Christ is not to be taken very seriously, and as a result she never feels any real urgency to submit to Christ's claims on her life.

We have seen a large number of these mixed marriages in which the non-Christian is attending church with the boyfriend or girlfriend during courtship and promises to continue after marriage. This doesn't last very long, however. After the novelty of marriage has worn off, the two of them don't feel a compulsion to go everywhere together anymore. They are no longer so eager to indulge each other's every whim. Besides, all that talk before the wedding was sort of like campaign promises. No one really takes them too seriously after the fact. So the Christian partner finds himself in a bad situation which shows no signs of improving.

One of the most dramatic stories of this kind was told me by a veteran minister's wife. A Christian girl married a non-Christian who had been attending church with her. He promised that he would join the church after they were married. Unlike most, he kept his promise about going to church, although he never became a member. Every Sunday, without fail, he attended worship services with his wife. Eventually they had children. All seemed to go well for almost twenty years.

Then gradually he stopped participating in the services. Since the church was in the liturgical tradition, his lack of participation was quite obvious. He was there in body, but clearly he was protesting. He never joined in the singing or participated in the liturgy in any way. Finally he stopped going to church altogether.

After a time his protest became more serious. He tried to talk his wife out of attending as well. When she refused to give up worshipping, one Sunday he forbade her to go.

This woman was the very model of a submissive wife. She respected her husband and was always gracious to him, even though he was argumentative, overbearing, and authoritarian. The whole community marvelled at how she coped with her situation. She also taught the children to respect their father. They never rebelled at his often arbitrary discipline.

But it was clear that a crucial choice had just been presented to her. She knew that her husband was trying to banish God from her life. She realized that if she stayed home this time, she would probably never go again. So she packed the children in the car and went. Her husband was so furious that he got in his car and tore off at a tremendous speed. He lost control of the car on a curve in the road, crashed, and was killed.

We have also seen happy instances in which a Christian led a person of the opposite sex to Christ because he or she refused to let their relationship become serious. I remember a very beautiful young girl who started attending our church. She was not a believer, but she was seeking. At one of the youth meetings she met a young man from the church who interested her. Occasionally he would drive her home from a meeting. They would always discuss things having to do with the Christian life.

Her interest in him grew, and became very frustrated that he never asked her for a date. She was not used to having her charms resisted. Finally she could stand it no longer. She asked him why he was keeping a distance between them, when it was obvious that he liked her. He explained that Christ was the most important person in his life and serving him was the one thing that mattered. She was not committed to Christ. So although he was very much attracted to her, he could not allow himself to become involved. It was as simple as that.

Well! She had never in her young life come up against anything like this. Competition from other girls she could handle. But this was something else. She was challenged as she never had been before. She determined to find out all she could about Christ. She enrolled in a course of instruction at the church. She did her homework and asked the teacher innumerable questions—many of them hard questions. Some time later, when the teacher presented the claims of Christ to her, she committed her life to Him.

When her friend saw that her life had, indeed, begun to change and that she was serious about her faith, they began to date. In time they became engaged.

The story has a happy ending, although it's not the classic storybook finish. Eventually they realized that they were not really suited for each other, in spite of their strong spiritual oneness. Their interests were too dissimilar. Although it was hard for them to break up, they realized that the Lord had other plans for them. He married a girl whose temperament was better suited to his; she married someone who shared her interests.

Although this was many years ago, we still keep in touch with this woman at Christmastime. She has never lost her wonder and joy at having been received into God's family. The community of believers is unlike anything she had ever experienced before.

In another instance a woman refused to become involved with a man who was not a Christian. He also was fascinated by the challenge and because of this found Christ. Again, although they dated for a while, they did not marry each other.

Developing a Relationship

Once you begin dating, there is a definite pattern which the relationship should follow. First it should begin to develop spiritually, then socially, and finally physically. The culture around us has this order just reversed. A recent incident involving a friend of mine is an extreme example of this foolishness. My friend, a beautiful woman, made a stop late one evening in a supermarket. As she was scanning the shelves for an item, a young man whom she had never seen before passed, stopped to look at her again, and then exclaimed, "I think I'm in love!" Obviously this could be no more than physical attraction. The woman had not even spoken to him.

In a typical dating situation a young man and a girl are attracted to each other physically, so they start to go out together. On their first dates they begin holding hands and kissing. As weeks and months go by, they usually get more and more physically involved. After they have been seeing each other steadily for several months—especially if they are old enough to start talking about marriage—most likely they have gotten into some pretty heavy petting.

Then, as they have been spending a lot of time with each other, they probably start to develop the social side of their relationship. They discover which interests they have in common, and get to know one another's likes and dislikes. Somewhere along the line they meet each other's families.

Finally, after they have become seriously involved with each other and have decided to marry, they may think about the spiritual implications of their life together. Perhaps they first discuss anything religious when they begin to think about which church they will go to after they get married. Will they be Baptists like her family, or Lutherans like his?

This is completely backwards. Christian young people should never fall into this trap. When they allow themselves to become physically involved with each other before they have discussed their commitment to Christ and their spiritual priorities, they find themselves in serious trouble. Often the fact of their physical involvement propels them into marriage, even though they are not right for each other. Their physical desire, which has been stimulated and encouraged all these months, cries out so loudly that any voices of reason are likely to be drowned out. They don't even realize the folly they are committing.

Or if they do discuss their goals and commitments before marriage, they may realize that they have some important, perhaps serious, differences. But by this time they feel caught. Because of their physical familiarity, they don't really feel that it would be right to break up. If they have actually had sexual intercourse, the guilt they feel is even greater.

Because the sex drive is so strong and can have such devastating effects, care must be taken to insure that the physical part of a relationship remains very low-key until the spiritual and social aspects are well developed. When a couple have talked over their priorities—as individuals and as a couple—they will be able to decide, rationally and unemotionally, how they will allow the physical aspect of their relationship to proceed. It will not just happen. They will be assuming responsibility for their actions.

This is not easy to do. It has never been easy. But it is particularly difficult today. In the culture in which we are living feelings have been elevated to a very high position. A song which was popular recently has a line which asks how something can be wrong when it feels so right. The implied answer is, of course, that because it feels so right it *must* be all right. We have probably all seen bumper stickers urging, "If it feels good, do it."

This advice is totally counter to the biblical message. God calls us to make decisions on the basis of His will for our lives. This may not "feel" as good at the time; but in the end it feels much better. I have talked to many couples who have disciplined themselves to the spiritual-social-physical order in their dating, and they all say that it makes them feel good about themselves.

One engaged couple who talked to me recently said that because they were first attracted to each other by their shared spiritual commitment, the physical has never been a big problem. After a couple of weeks of dating they decided on some basic rules. One of these was that they would never sit in the car together after a date. Discussing their decision with me they said, "We feel so free. Now that we know what to expect from each other, it eliminates the agonizing. We can now get on with really learning to know each other, without the pressure of the physical thing always getting in the way."

Spiritual Priorities

Having decided to set spiritual priorities together, where do you begin? In the first place, it is important that the two of you have the same level of commitment. One or the other may be farther along in his Christian life. That is not so important. What is important is that both partners are equally committed—both to Christ and to the ministry. If a man is all excited about opportunities to serve and his wife does not share his enthusiasm, it is going to be uphill all the way, even though she is a Christian.

It is vital that the implications of the ministry be discussed together beforehand in as much detail as is necessary and agreement be reached on as many specifics as possible. There are plenty of unknowns to be encountered. At least the givens of the ministry should be thoroughly talked out ahead of time. If the woman you are planning to marry has any reservations about the ministry, it is imperative that these be faced and dealt with. Do not let the stars in your eyes blind you at this point. Her worries may be unfounded. Perhaps solutions for her concerns can be agreed upon satisfactorily before marriage. But if you sense a lack of commitment, don't go any further! If you do, you will have nothing but trouble. Many of the divorced pastors whom I interviewed said that their ex-wives had not had the same level of commitment that they had, and in the end the marriages broke up.

Similar Level of Education

Another theme which runs clearly through all the interviews I took is that ministerial marriages are far healthier when the husband and wife have roughly the same level of education. In fact, in the nearly two hundred personal, hour-long interviews I conducted, there were virtually no exceptions to this rule.

Once I thought I had found an exception. I was interviewing the wife of a highly successful minister who served a large, growing congregation. I knew of his ministry from friends who are members of his congregation and from things I had read about the church. As we were talking, this wife told me that she had never even finished high school. Aha, I thought. Here is the exception that proves the rule. It was obvious that this couple had an excellent marriage. They discussed important issues together, and she was a great asset in the ministry.

Then as I went down the line with my questions, I discovered that her husband had also dropped out of high school and had had no more formal education since. He was serving in a denomination which required neither college nor seminary for entrance into the ministry. But they read books on theology, on the Christian experience, and any other subjects which they thought might be helpful. Together they had become quite educated outside of the usual structures. But again, as in other successful marriages, the level of education was approximately the same.

Of course marriages can fail in spite of a shared educational experience. It is just that this is something the good ones all seem to have in common. Someone has said that all happy families are alike, but each of the unhappy ones is unhappy in its own way.

So if you are planning to go through college and seminary, by all means choose a woman who has graduated from college or who plans to. The conclusion I came to was that when their wives were not approximately as educated as they, the men did not really feel that they could talk things over with them. Consequently, the women were not able to share significantly in their husbands' lives. They grew apart, and the women, particularly, became increasingly more frustrated.

Of course when a minister and his wife find themselves in this situation, it is not hopeless. There are several ways in which to compensate. We will talk about this in chapter 9. No problem is too big for the Lord. But it is not responsible to go into marriage with unnecessary problems. Since marriage in the parsonage has its own set of potential problems built in, there is no sense in adding another before you even begin.

Order of Priorities for Education and Marriage

It also seems to work out best to postpone marriage at least until you are both finished with college. I still think that it is ideal to wait until you are almost through seminary to be married. If your seminary has an internship program, this year could be a good time to be married.

My husband and I met while he was in his last year of seminary and were married during his first year of graduate work. He had enough money saved up for graduate school, so I never had to get a job to support him.

However, I realize that this is not usual. Even then, twenty-one years ago, he was one of only three of his classmates who were single at graduation from seminary. And since we had just met in his last year, we didn't have to go through a long dating period. I speeded up my college program to graduate early, so we were married a year after we met.

It does not always work out that nicely. If you were to meet a girl in your freshman year, for instance, and realize that she was the one God meant for you to marry, it would probably be very difficult to wait for your education to be completed before you would marry.

It would be easiest not to meet your future wife right away! But since that may not be practical, at least try to wait until you have completed college to marry. Remember, you still have three or four years of seminary ahead of you.

Bill Gothard advocates postponing marriage until you are financially independent. That way you will never have to depend on your wife to support you. I agree that this is ideal. I also realize that in many cases it may be very difficult to achieve.

However, having children can be postponed until you are through seminary. If you start a family immediately, your wife will probably not be able to be the family breadwinner. That forces you to support your growing family in addition to going to school.

This can be done, usually by stretching the course work over an extra year or so. But you will sacrifice many, if not all, extracurricular activities, and your study time will probably be curtailed also. You will have no time for the after hours discussions around a cup of coffee that are part of student life and part of your educational experience. You will not feel as if you are in the mainstream of student life, because you will be rushing from classes to work and then rushing home again.

The very real temptation will be to do your studying simply with an eye to passing your courses with the required grades so that you can graduate. You won't really have time to try to learn all you can. School then becomes somewhat of an endurance course. You will begin your ministry with a better education and far less hampered by financial pressures if you give your education priority before starting a family.

Special Circumstances

Many feel that the Lord is calling them into the ministry when they are older than the average college or seminary student. Often they have been in business or another profession for a number of years. Usually these men are already married and have their children.

If you are one of these men, you no doubt realize that your entire family will be called upon to make special sacrifices during your college and seminary years. Your standard of living will probably be greatly reduced. Most likely your wife will have to take a job outside the home, and probably your teenagers will need part-time jobs, also. All expenditures which are not strictly necessary may have to be eliminated, including new clothes, fast food restaurants, movies, etc.

Before you make the momentous decision to leave the career with which you and your family are familiar, I beg you to discuss it at length with your entire family. Be particularly careful to get as much input as you can from your wife and to weigh it carefully. Listen to what she says, and try very carefully to learn how she both thinks and feels about the proposed change. Remember, this is going to affect her as totally as it affects you. At this point you are no longer free to make major decisions alone. When you were young and single, your career choice was between you and God. Now you are married and your commitment is first of all to your wife and then to a profession. Even such a high calling as the ministry may not come before your marriage. If you feel that the Lord is calling you to the ministry, but your wife is not wholeheartedly with you, I believe the Lord is not calling you.

If you go ahead in spite of your wife's reluctance, at best, you will not be as effective a pastor as you had hoped. At worst, your ministry will be sabotaged and your marriage shipwrecked.

You may be able to talk your wife into agreeing with you concerning the ministry. After all, she loves you and wants you to be happy. More than that, she is committed to promoting your well-being. She is also deeply committed to God. Who is she to stand in the way if you feel that God is calling you into the ministry? You can see what a bind she is in. If she opposes you she feels that she is displeasing and disappointing both her husband and God. How can a woman live with that on her conscience? So she may go along with your decision, even though she has grave doubts about being able to handle the situation. She is not being phony. She really tries to convince herself that it will work out. She *has* to convince herself. Her well-being and peace of mind are at stake. So she tries to quiet her doubts.

Things will probably go well during seminary. The whole family will rise to the occasion and pull together. But after your wife has been in the parsonage a few years, her doubts may surface again. She will miss her old friends who may now be a thousand miles away. She may resent having to live on a reduced income but feel guilty about it. Her previous fears about not having the gifts to be a minister's wife seem to be justified. And in addition, there is the pressure of trying to be something that she feels she is not.

She now feels failure, guilt for that failure (a better person would have succeeded), and resentment against you for pushing her into the whole thing. This is an explosive situation which many marriages have not survived. So be sure that you are correctly assessing your wife's response and not putting words in her mouth. Remember, this is your wife's life as well as yours.

Chapter 8

Words to Wives and Girlfriends of Seminarians

When I was in high school, one of my teachers used to tell her students that being a minister's wife was a career that some of us should be training for. We pretended to listen in class, but privately we had a good laugh about the idea. We thought it a highly fanciful, rather silly idea of a frustrated old maid. Twenty-some years later the idea still seems as impractical as ever. After all, one certainly cannot finish a certain course of study and then apply for the position of minister's wife.

This teacher was on to something, however. Whether or not we like it, the minister's wife does have a special position both in the church and in the community. Although there are signs that it is weakening, the stereotype of the minister's wife is still with us, more so in certain areas and certain churches than in others. To be forewarned is to be forearmed. In a later chapter answers to this problem will be discussed more thoroughly.

In the meantime there are ways in which young women can prepare themselves to be ministers' wives.

Commitment to a Man, Not a Job

First of all, commitment is to a man and not to his job. Obviously most women understand that. And yet there are a few women around who are very much taken with the idea of being a minister's wife. It doesn't much matter who the man is as long as he is going into the ministry. No, they would never admit that to anyone—

perhaps not even to themselves. But they just do not seem to be attracted to other men. I call them the "professional ministers' wives." When one of these women does marry a minister, that marriage often becomes a disaster.

My husband talked to the ex-husband of one of these women not long ago. Ever since she was a young girl, Nadine had wanted to marry a minister. When she and Bill were married, everyone— including the pastor who married them—talked about what a perfect minister's wife she would make.

For many years she seemed to be just that. She did all the prescribed things. She led Bible studies, coordinated potlucks, visited the people in the congregation, sang in the choir, and played the piano for Sunday school. She even had a Sunday school class meeting in her living room every week. She was constantly busy. Everyone in the church seemed to like her. People commented about how dedicated she was.

When her husband had an affair with another woman and left the ministry, the whole congregation was shocked. But from her husband's point of view, she was more in love with her role than with him. It sounded like the flip side of the "man married to his career" theme. Church work always came ahead of him. She had little time for her husband. And finally, their sex life dwindled down to nothing. Since his self-esteem had also taken a battering at the hands of the church board recently, Bill was very vulnerable to the charms of another woman who set out to get him. Bill and Nadine are now divorced, and he is married to the woman who had time for him—who made him feel that he was first in her life.

I believe that a woman can be called to be a minister's wife. But she must always remember that her primary calling is to be a wife to a man. In their relationship he is first of all a man and a husband; second, a minister. If while filling the job description she has for herself as a minister's wife (or perhaps that the congregation has set up for her) she forgets to be a wife, she is in trouble.

Curt and Cindy

Recently I interviewed a young girl who is engaged to a pre-sem student. The daughter of a minister, she had always wanted to be a minister's wife like her mother. Then she met and started dating a young man who was not planning to go into the ministry. As their relationship developed, it gradually seemed as if the Lord had picked them out for each other. Both of them were committed to dating only young people who were excited about their faith. In their very first conversation they realized that their spiritual goals were the same. They were both eager to share their faith with others and wanted their lives to count for God.

As they continued dating, they found that socially they had a lot in common also. Their backgrounds were very similar, and they shared many interests. Both were good students, and they enjoyed discussing a wide variety of ideas together.

Then came the day of reckoning. Curt asked Cindy to marry him. At this point she had a real struggle. Although she had been very careful never to even hint at it to Curt, Cindy had always felt that God had planned for her to be a minister's wife. And yet she felt Curt was the right man for her to marry. She talked to her parents about it, agonized, prayed, and cried. Finally she came to the point where she said, "All right God, this is obviously the man you want me to marry, so I guess you don't want me to be a minister's wife after all."

At that point something very interesting started to happen. Curt's best friend, his dorm advisor, and his pastor, each without the other's knowledge, suggested to Curt that perhaps he should consider the ministry as a possibility. They all pointed out that he had many of the necessary gifts. He was eager to share his faith and had been used to introduce some of his friends to Christ. He was also a sympathetic listener—people tended to tell him their problems, often on the first meeting. And he seemed to have some talent for giving good counsel. All of the classes he had taken in college so far could apply to a pre-sem course, so he would not lose any time.

Now it was Curt's turn to agonize, pray, and carefully weigh pros and cons. One of the professors whom he consulted pointed out that his girlfriend also had many gifts which could help him in his ministry.

By the end of that school year Curt had decided that, indeed, the Lord was calling him into the ministry. So after Cindy had made her commitment to Curt to simply be his wife, she found out that the Lord was evidently going to allow her to be a minister's wife as well. Cindy feels that the whole experience was a learning one for her, because she was forced to get her priorities straight.

Importance of Education

Secondly, if you are planning to marry a minister, finish your own education first. A repetitive theme throughout my many interviews was that couples seemed to have far better marriages when the husbands and wives had approximately equivalent educations.

This was expected of course. This trend holds true for marriages in general and not only for clergy marriages. Most people are familiar with the outgrown wife syndrome in which the wife sacrifices her own education to go to work and support her husband through medical school, law school or other graduate studies, only to find when it's all over that she can no longer effectively communicate with her husband. Replete with his newly acquired expertise, he finds her dull and boring and prefers to talk and visit with colleagues or others in his ever-widening social circle.

But somehow I had not expected ministers' wives to be in the ranks of the "outgrown wives." I was wrong. Evidently spirituality does not necessarily substitute for education. So if your husband-to-be is a college graduate and plans to go to seminary, by all means get a college education yourself, if at all possible.

One obviously bright woman mentioned that she would often beg her husband to converse with her about his work, but he never would. Understandably, she felt he didn't consider her opinions to be worth anything. He had gone through seminary and also had a doctorate, while she had given up her college plans to marry him.

A college education is not simply training for a job. Today's college degree doesn't automatically give someone an edge on the job market. But a college education, particularly a good liberal arts education, prepares a person to go on learning for the rest of his life. It opens doors to the world's knowledge. Once you have graduated from college you will have increased your store of knowledge a bit. But far more important, you will have the necessary tools to go on learning.

A college degree will also enhance your self-esteem. You will feel more confident about meeting people in various occupations and professions. This is particularly important for a minister's wife. Even though you may have a terrific self-image, there are enough stresses and strains already built into parsonage life, so there's no sense giving yourself a handicap.

In one of the previous interviews I mentioned an ex-minister's wife who felt displaced after the husband accepted a call to be a campus minister. She had always done a lot of entertaining in the parsonage, but since she hadn't gone to college, she felt uncomfortable around students and seldom invited them over. As a result she began to develop totally separate interests from her husband's and they drifted apart. Obviously being unable to share in his work on the campus contributed to their breakup.

Special Circumstances for Wives

The chapter to seminarians dealt with men who had been businessmen, engineers, or farmers for a number of years before they felt God's calling to the ministry. Being married to one of these men presents a special challenge. Patient and persistent prayer, along with much discussion between husband and wife, should precede any decision to change careers. This is a joint decision. Make no mistake about it. You are in this together.

As you consider this new venture, you will encounter many apprehensions. This is natural. In order to better understand what you are getting into, I suggest talking to your pastor and his wife. They will be able to give you a realistic idea of what is involved in being a pastor's wife.

Comparing yourself with your pastor's wife, however, is inadvisable. If you do, you will probably decide that you don't measure up. She may or may not be older than you, but certainly she is more experienced. She may also have gifts that you do not have. On the other hand, you may have the same gifts, but you may not have had the opportunity to use them, so they are as yet undeveloped.

No one has precisely the same ministry. For example, perhaps your pastor's wife has always taught a Sunday school class. That does not mean that you should be a Sunday school teacher. God may be planning something quite different for you. If you are open to what God has for you and you rely on Him for strength and grace, you will be effective.

This doesn't mean that God will simply give you the ability to grin and bear it. If your husband and you have carefully and prayerfully come to the decision that the ministry is for you, you can proceed with the knowledge that you are in God's will. And as you proceed, you will find a great sense of fulfillment.

Although I had never planned to be a minister's wife, I wouldn't now trade places with anyone. Before I met my husband no one would have dreamed that I would marry a minister. So my friends were quite surprised when I announced my engagement to a seminary student. I suppose few people would have felt me well qualified for the job. The resources I possessed, however, were a strong Christian family and upbringing, a solid religious education, and many years of training on both piano and organ. Incidentally, my musical training is probably the only resource which fits the picture of the stereotyped minister's wife. Actually, my husband has often wished that I were a typist instead of a musician, since we have seldom lacked for piano players or organists.

Although I did not feel particularly qualified to be a minister's wife, I went into it with a sense of adventure, learning a lot along the way. Even though I have been known to go to the corner store barefooted, and my wardrobe would definitely not please some of the good ladies who give advice on such matters, the Lord has blessed my ministry.

You yourself may have personality quirks which seem improper for a pastor's wife. If your behavior is not unbiblical and is not hurting anyone, don't worry about it. The Lord will use your individual personality just the way you are.

Of course, if you are behaving or dressing in a certain way out of rebellion, even if it is not conscious rebellion, your ministry will be short-circuited. Once in a while one encounters a person in a position of spiritual leadership who, in a certain sense, hasn't grown up. He still has the attitude of a tough kid. He has a hard time accepting authority and wants to be unconventional just to thumb his nose at the establishment. This type of person will often gain a following, at least at first, because negative power is easy to grab. If you are against something, you can always find a few other people who will be against it with you. Young people in particular will often be attracted to this kind of leader—at least for a time. However, this is not real leadership; a true leader gives positive direction.

If your attitude is right, and you are truly trying to find and do God's will, you can create your own style as a pastor's wife. We'll go into the specifics of how this can be accomplished in chapter 10.

Chapter 9

Words to Pastors

Talking to pastors about marriage is a bit like giving medical advice to doctors. After all, ministers do a large share of the marriage counseling in the country today. They are the experts. But even experts sometimes have problems. There is more than a grain of truth in the old adage which says "the shoemaker's children go unshod." My own experience tells me that piano teachers' children often have their lessons skipped. And through these interviews it has become evident that ministers' families sometimes suffer from neglect.

Many pastors' wives feel that they and the children take second place to the church. And perhaps some pastors think that this is as it should be. I have read a number of books for ministers' wives which tell us that we must accept this as part of our suffering for Christ—that a minister should never let his home life interfere with his work for the Lord.

What the people who give this advice fail to see is that a man's family is also part of his work for the Lord; furthermore, it is his primary responsibility. If he fails in his family relationships, he might as well forget the high calling of the ministry. Paul says in 1 Timothy 3:4, 5 that an elder or a minister must "manage his own household well . . . for if a man does not know how to manage his own household, how can he care for God's church?" So if you fail with your family, you fail to qualify to be a minister. It's as simple as that.

In the chapter defining marriage we discussed the husband's responsibility as head in the marriage. Every husband has this role. But there are special areas of leadership for a husband who is also a pastor.

Encourage Your Wife to Use Her Gifts

Each Christian has at least one spiritual gift, as we know from Scripture. This will be discussed further in the next chapter. It is up to you, as a husband, to encourage your wife to use her gift or gifts. Perhaps she will need help to discover just what these are. She may be, like many Christians, leading a rather humdrum spiritual life simply because she doesn't realize how much more God could be using her.

As a minister, there is not much chance that your spiritual gifts will long go undetected. The ministry usually forces you to exercise any gifts and talents that you have plus a few that you only wish you had. Sometimes this is true of the minister's wife also. But in a sizable number of cases the minister's wife is kept very busy tending to tasks that have little to do with her real gifts and abilities. If she spends all of her available time organizing potlucks and baking cookies for bazaars, how will she know whether or not she has a gift for teaching, or perhaps evangelism? You can help her by supporting her as she tries her wings in different areas.

Protect Her from Trivia

In order to support your wife as she discovers and develops her spiritual gifts, you must protect her from wasting her energies doing things that are not in line with her real gifts. If she does not have a talent for organization, there is no reason that she should coordinate committees, even though all of the previous pastors' wives did this. They, too, may have been doing it only because it was expected of them. By the same token, not all ministers' wives have the gift of helps, so why should they always be expected to be in the kitchen at any church function? If your wife shines in this area and feels called to serve in the kitchen—great. Support her as she makes her contribution in this way. But if this is not her thing, help her to say "no." After all, there are many lay women who need to be involved in the different aspects of running the church. If your wife knows that you are behind her when she declines a certain job, it will minimize her feelings of guilt. Your support will not necessarily wipe out her guilt feelings, but it will go a long way toward alleviating them.

In some cases the person or group asking your wife to do a certain job may not take her "no" for an answer. Some laymen with very definite ideas about the fitness of things feel that it is incumbent on them to spell out the duties of the minister's wife for her. A person like this can be very hard to deal with, particularly if he or she is older than your wife. Even if he is not older, he may have been a member of this particular congregation longer and so feel that he knows how things should go here. In this case you, as a husband, must (as tactfully as possible, of course) confront the person yourself and tell him that you are not allowing your wife to take on this task at this time.

It is much easier for you to say "no" for your wife in a case like this than for her to do it herself. If this is pulling rank, then so be it. If your wife is going to function effectively in her multiple role of wife, mother, and pastor's wife, she needs all the help she can get.

Recently a group in our congregation asked my husband to volunteer me for a certain job which he knew I would really dislike. He told them that he wasn't even going to ask me, because he knew it was not something which I should be doing. Since this specific job would have given me quite an emotional trauma, I was very pleased that my husband had protected me in this way.

Get Her Involved in Your Life

It might sound a little silly to tell you to get your wife involved with you. How can she *not* be involved with you? She's your wife, isn't she?

A disconcerting number of the interviews show that this is not necessarily the case. Your wife may be very involved in the church, all right, but from quite a different angle. She needs to be involved in what you are doing.

This doesn't mean that she has to do everything with you. But there are many different aspects of your work that you can discuss with her. Obviously she can't write your sermons or deliver them. But she can help you think through some of the themes in your sermon preparation. If you're struggling with the development of a concept, try it out on your wife.

Another area in which the two of you can function as a couple is in visiting and counseling. The extent of your wife's involvement will be determined by how busy she is with home management duties and by her inclination and gifts for counseling. Some husbands take their wives along only on routine (nonproblem) visits to people in the congregation. Others like them along on hospital visits and even crisis counseling.

One thing has become clear from my research: those marriages do best in which there is some degree of visiting done together. One statement kept repeating itself throughout the interviews with ex-ministers' wives: "I would ask him to take me along when he went visiting, but he never would." Or, "I would have liked to be involved in some of his counseling, but he shut me out. He would never discuss anything with me."

The best marriages seemed to be the ones in which the husband treated his wife as his chief confidante. Obviously there are certain things that you are not allowed to share with your wife. And of course she must understand that confidences are not to be shared with others. But you will find that your wife's advice can be very helpful on many occasions. And your relationship will be enhanced.

Encourage Her in Her Education

We have seen that the best clergy marriages seem to be the ones in which the wife has roughly the same amount of education as the husband. If this is not the case in your home, there is no need to despair. If you are newly married, or have no children, or if your children are grown and have left home, perhaps you could encourage your wife to enroll in college part time. Today most colleges and universities are geared to include people of all ages, many of whom have been out of school for a number of years.

You could encourage her to include courses which would develop her gifts and enhance her ministry along with you. If you are fortunate enough to live in an area where there is a seminary, she might take a course or two there. Most of us don't have ready access to seminaries. However, college and seminary extension courses are often available. One of the country's leading seminaries has offered extension courses in our city for several years. Two of our local pastors' wives have taken a number of these courses and have found them to be helpful in their ministry.

Of course college is not the only place where education is acquired. In fact, the knowledge acquired during four years of college is only a small fraction of the total knowledge which a person accumulates during his lifetime. And the facts and skills gained in college are not necessarily the most important of all, even if one has attended an excellent school. What a college does, if it is doing its job properly, is something far better than imparting bits and pieces of wisdom. The right sort of college gives the student a start toward real learning; it gives him a taste of the world's intellectual riches plus the desire and the tools with which to go on learning.

If college is out of the question for your wife, you can encourage her to learn on her own and with you. A way to start might be with a current religious book that you would like to read. You could read it and discuss it together. This could be a book on marriage, counseling, or child raising, for example. Obviously you are not going to start with heavy theology. After you have done a few books together, your wife will probably also continue a program of reading on her own.

Attend Conferences Together

Another way to learn is to attend some of the various seminars and mini-courses which are offered in such abundance today. Sometimes there is a registration fee for these lectures or courses, but often they are free. If you and your wife can attend some of these seminars together, you will receive the additional benefit of growing in these specific areas together.

Many pastors attend all kinds of interesting conferences without their wives. This can contribute to their drifting apart. Most church boards and others who schedule these retreats and conferences now encourage the wives to attend as well as the husbands. They realize that it is important for the couple to share these experiences.

My husband and I would never have developed our common interest in evangelism if we had not gone to several seminars together. During the few days away together we would discuss the new material and ideas which had been presented to us. After this refreshing time together we would be inspired again for our ministry. We would set goals together to try out some of the new ideas and then begin implementing those goals.

The mission board for which my husband works schedules annual four-day conferences which both husbands and wives are required to attend. There are workshops and discussions on teaching, preaching, counseling, and other aspects of ministry. We have also discussed husband-wife relationships. In all of these sessions the wives are absolutely equal participants, which we really appreciate.

And we can make significant contributions to the discussions.

The board has periodically examined its policy because of the expense involved in sending two people from each family instead of one. They have concluded that it is a responsible use of the Lord's money to let their missionaries share these experiences as couples.

In addition to the material presented, there are opportunities for socializing and sharing experiences with colleagues. This aspect of the conferences is perhaps as important as the formal agenda. We have a chance to bear one another's burdens and to encourage each other.

Take Responsibility for Child-Rearing

One of the few complaints that I heard regularly from pastors' wives about their husbands was that they didn't see enough of them. They often felt they were left to cope by themselves with most of the problems of running the parsonage. This was most keenly felt in the area of child-rearing.

Bringing up children demands a sizable commitment of time and emotional energy if it is to be done the way God wants us to do it. This subject will be enlarged upon in chapter 11. Commitment must come from both the father and the mother. It is not fair to the child or children for the father to abdicate his responsibility. The absence of fathers in many ghetto families is evident to everyone. The results are much the same in "nice" middle-class families when the father is absent much of the time and leaves the decision-making to the mother.

The point I want to make is the unfairness to your wife when you put the larger share of responsibility for child-rearing on her shoulders. She needs you to give direction in making major decisions which affect the children. These decisions should be made by the two of you; you are both responsible for guiding your children. However, you as leader must give direction.

The Bible makes it clear that fathers are to take responsibility for the nurture of their children. Ephesians 6:4 says, "Fathers, do not provoke your children to anger, but bring them up in the discipline and instruction of the Lord." [15] Paul gives much the same advice in Colossians 3:21, adding a note warning fathers to watch that their children don't become discouraged from too much criticism.

Deuteronomy 6:6-9 reads, "And these words which I command you this day shall be upon your heart; and you shall teach them diligently to your children, and talk of them when you sit in your house, and when you walk by the way, and when you lie down, and when you rise." [16] Since this injunction was given to Israel, we can be sure that it was not meant for mothers only! In fact, when directives were given to the people in the Old Testament, often they were meant specifically for the men.

Your wife may also need your physical help with the children, especially when they are young and active. Perhaps part of your day off each week should be devoted to taking care of the babies while your wife has a little time to herself. After all, does she have a day off? It is extremely important to do things together as a family, but it is also important for your wife to *regularly* have some time all by herself. When the last one starts school she will have that time, but as long as she has a preschooler, her time is really never free. She certainly loves her children, and she may very much enjoy her role as mother. But that does not mean that she enjoys doing it twenty-four hours a day without a break. Remember, they are your children just as much as they are hers! She is in the ministry with you, and you are in the child-rearing business with her.

I am sure that one of the reasons homemakers have been leaving their homes in such large numbers in recent years is that they have become sick and tired of having to do all of the housework and child-rearing by themselves, often without so much as a "thank-you." And women in the parsonage are subject to more stresses and strains than the average homemaker. I recently read the results of a study which claimed that of all professions, the ministry and the medical profession were harder on the wives than on the men themselves. A little help from husbands could do a lot to improve this situation.

I must raise a word of caution here, however. Helping a mother with small children to have a little time to herself is one thing. But baby-sitting and doing housework because your wife has a job outside the home is quite another. If the congregation is paying you a salary for a full-time job, it is not honest to take part of that time to do work that your wife would be doing if she were not out working elsewhere. This is cheating the congregation. It is easy to fall into this sort of thing, because you have no one dictating your daily job description. Your time is usually your own to schedule. It is not right to baby-sit or do housework during hours in which you would otherwise be doing your regular work.

Of course it is a different matter if you are in a situation in which the congregation cannot pay you a full salary. In this case you cannot be expected to give all of your working hours to the church.

Time Management

At first glance time management may seem to be an odd subject appearing in a book on marriage. But since pastors' wives so often shared their concerns over lack of time together as couples and as families, it seemed wise to include a discussion of time management principles in this book.

Define Your Job

A good way to begin organizing your time is to define your job. There is no way to effectively set goals and establish priorities unless you can define your job. So many of us bumble along from day to day doing whatever comes to hand, or—and this is probably true of most pastors—doing whatever demands our attention most insistently. As a result we're always busy getting a number of things accomplished, and we feel quite virtuous because we're working so hard. However, as Ted Engstrom says in World Vision time management seminars, it's not how much you do that counts, but how much you get done. Perhaps much of what you're doing doesn't really need doing. If it does, perhaps someone else could be doing it.

Most pastors have no supervisor to hand them a specific job description. There are many assumptions about the job of pastoring, but few particulars are ever spelled out. Generally, the pastor must decide for himself exactly what his job is.

Does it include preaching, teaching, counseling, and attending meetings? As you begin to define your job, start with the givens which are not negotiable such as preparing the sermon, preaching on Sunday morning, and meeting with your board of deacons or elders. Add to this list presiding at weddings and funerals of members and any other activities which are absolutely built into your job. But be honest—the fact that you are presently doing a certain chore does not mean it is necessarily a part of your job.

At this point you have a bare bones outline of your job. You can now start adding the activities which seem to be necessary to enable the church to be carrying out *its* job, provided these activities fit your talents and really are best performed by you. This brings us to two other aspects of time management: goal-setting and delegating.

Importance of Goals

In order to properly perform any task, you have to have a goal. If you don't know where you're going, how will you know whether or not you've reached your destination?

Your goals as pastor should, of course, fit in with the goals of your church. Probably you have helped the church to define its goals. Does your church have a teaching ministry? Is community outreach one of its objectives? Does it aim to minister to troubled people in the community?

Once you have taken a look at the goals of your church, you can begin to figure out exactly what your job should be. If evangelism is a main emphasis in your church and you have the gift of evangelism, you will probably want to give leadership in this area. If teaching is important to your church's ministry, you will probably be doing quite a bit of teaching.

A word of warning, however. While you are defining your job, be sure that you describe a man-sized job. By that I mean a job which a man can reasonably be expected to do. If you try to do all the teaching, all the counseling, all the evangelizing, all the preaching, and anything else that seems to be required of you, you won't do a great job in any of the areas, besides feeling frustrated much of the time. Your family life will also suffer. So take a sober, honest look at how much you can actually expect to do in your working hours, and plan accordingly. The rest of the work will simply have to be done by someone else—preferably many others.

Get Laymen Involved

This brings us to another of the important principles of time management: delegate, delegate, delegate! The best managers (and as a pastor you are a manager) are the ones who get things done through others. Ed Dayton says there are three kinds of things you should delegate to others: "those things you can't do because you really don't know how, . . . those things others can do better, . . . and those things you shouldn't be doing because they aren't part of your primary goals. . . ." [17] This is excellent advice. However, in the case of the pastor I would have to add a fourth category: delegate some of the things which you *do* know how to do and which no one really can do better, but which you do not have enough time for. Unlike managers in business, you are not in charge of employees who were hired for their experience and skills in furthering company goals. You have church members who may or may not have any helpful experience and/or skills. But they can learn.

This involves training. You cannot simply tell a person to go out and do something that he does not know how to do. Training also involves planning and goal-setting. It often seems easier to simply keep on doing a thing ourselves than to take the time and effort to train someone else to do it. Probably there are even ego rewards in feeling indispensable. After all, look at all the things we're doing that no one else can do! Of course we don't actually say that to ourselves in so many words, but the psychic rewards are there.

Ephesians 4:11, 12 reads, "And his [Christ's] gifts were that some should be . . . pastors and teachers, to equip the saints for the work of ministry, for building up the body of Christ." Paul seems to be telling us here that pastors and teachers are to equip the laymen to do the work of ministry. Certainly the message of the New Testament is clear: all members are to do the work of Christ's church on earth. No one who knows the Scriptures would argue that the minister is to do the work of the church all by himself. Acts 1:8 tells us that we are all witnesses. Both Romans 12 and 1 Corinthians 12 tell us that each member of the body is necessary and useful—that each Christian has a spiritual gift.

And yet laymen often need help in discovering just what their gifts are as well as training to use those gifts. Training church members does take an initial effort of time and energy from you as a pastor. But the rewards of training are great both for you and for your people. You will get the support which you so badly need, and your members will experience an added dimension to their life in Christ as they uncover and begin using gifts which they didn't know they had.

Paul Benjamin in his provocative article, "The Urgency of the Equipping Ministry" tells us that the concept of the equipping ministry (pastors teaching and preparing their laymen to do ministry) stems from the life and work of Jesus himself. First of all, Jesus found others to minister. "On the other hand, he turned some away because they could not meet the stringent demands of work in the kingdom (Luke 9:57-62). Jesus also equipped others to minister by loving them (John 13:1), by teaching them (Matt. 5:2), by praying

110

for them (Luke 22:39) and by training them on the job (Matt. 10:5, Luke 10:1). . . . The mission of the twelve and the seventy gives us crucial insight . . . Jesus equipped others to have a ministry of their own. . . .

"The apostle Paul also practiced an equipping ministry. . . . He surrounded himself with those who could later go out on their own. . . . [he] found potential leaders as he traveled from city to city. In many cases, they were invited to accompany him, learning as they traveled. Later on, they were directed to their own place of ministry. . . .

"The work of the preaching minister takes on new lustre when he is fulfilling his rightful vocation. . . . He is a "professional" in the best sense of the word. His work now is to set about helping others in the congregation to minister." [18]

Once you have a core (however small) of capable, responsible laymen working with you, you will have more time for your family. You will also be more relaxed and less preoccupied when you do spend time with them, because some of the responsibility has been taken from you.

Dealing with Women

Since a fair amount of broken clergy marriages today result from an improper handling of pastoral relationships with women, we must recognize that a problem exists. The fact that you as a pastor are in the Lord's work does not mean that you are above sexual temptation. In fact, your job may actually give rise to more temptations than most other men face.

The first step in solving the problem is to look at the factors which work to create it. One factor is that when counseling a woman, you are filling a very important need in her life. You are offering her wisdom, strength and understanding, all of which qualities are highly valued in a mate. If the counselee is a married woman, these may be just the qualities which at this point her husband seems not to possess at all. All of this is communicated to you in one way or another.

You must be alert to the fact that being needed is a very nice feeling. In fact, it may fill an important need in *your* life. If you are aware of this fact and will face it squarely, you can deal with it. After all, the purpose of pastoral counseling is not to meet your own needs. These are to be met in your own marriage and family life.

You are more vulnerable to the charms of another woman when your marriage relationship is not at its best. But you are responsible for your marriage. If you feel that your wife is not meeting your needs the way she should, it is up to you to see to it that the two of you work this out together. Perhaps your wife is not aware of certain needs in your life because you never let her know about them. Even the most perceptive wife cannot be expected to sense all of your needs without any help from you.

Perhaps she is being strong because you expect her to be—because you need a strong wife to help you. Then it is extremely unfair of you to put her in the position of competing with a woman whose very allure lies in the fact that she is weak.

Several ex-wives whom I interviewed exemplified the strong woman who lost her husband to a clinging-vine type. Esther was a striking example. Although she obviously was talented at the time that she got married, her husband was largely responsible for the strong woman that she is today. He encouraged, challenged, and pushed her—forcing her to gain competence in many areas of ministry. He demanded that she work as hard as he, which was very hard indeed. Because she had to, she became an excellent teacher, speaker, and hostess. She served as chairman of numerous committees and gained managerial skills. She learned to cope with nearly anything that came her way. And then, after twenty-some years of marriage and hard work alongside her husband, she lost him to a woman who couldn't seem to cope at all. This is not only quite ironic; it is also grossly unfair.

Another factor in the problem of pastor-counselee relationships with women is that, as we have seen, you are usually seeing the woman at her best physically and socially. Most likely she is nicely dressed and carefully made-up. Any woman possessing a shred of vanity is careful of her appearance when she has an appointment with a man. And she will also be on her best behavior. She may scream at her husband like a fish-wife, but she has her company manners on for you. Although she may be emotionally distraught, this does not make her unattractive. It just makes her appeal to your protective instinct.

So how will you handle this potentially dangerous situation? The first thing to do is to rely on the Holy Spirit. Pray before your counseling sessions, and turn the whole matter over to the Lord. If you are trying to find God's will for the counselee—really looking out for her best interests—the sessions will stay on a spiritual level where they belong. Certainly it is neither God's will nor in the woman's best interests that you become physically involved with her. Adultery is obviously never God's will, and by the same token it is never in a person's best interests to lead him or her into sin.

We have to realize that we are dealing here with the tremendous and subtle power of sin. Illicit sex has always been one of the devil's best weapons. It is good to keep in mind Paul's warning in Ephesians 6:12 that "we are not contending against flesh and blood, but against the principalities, against the powers, against the world rulers of this present darkness, against the spiritual hosts of wickedness in the heavenly places." If you approach the sessions in this manner, wearing the whole armor of God, you have a guarantee that things will not go wrong.

Although relying on the Holy Spirit, it is still up to you to act responsibly and with discretion in your counseling. In order to achieve this, it is wise to set up certain rules for yourself which you will not violate, no matter what.

The first of these would probably be to set a time limit on all sessions. Perhaps this will be no longer than an hour once a week. Maybe you will allow an hour and a half. Whatever your limit, let the counselee know about it ahead of time. Then when the time is up, be firm about stopping. Perhaps when the hour is almost gone you could look at your watch and mention that you have only a few more minutes. If you find breaking off the sessions difficult to achieve, you can purposely schedule something immediately afterward so that you must get up and leave.

Along with a time limit on the sessions, some counselors make a rule limiting phone calls between sessions to brief, businesslike calls to change or cancel an appointment.

Discretion during the sessions is also the better part of valor. You may want to schedule your sessions during times when you know that your secretary or someone else will be working in the next room, rather than at times when the two of you would be alone in the building.

In marriage counseling it is usually wise to see the husband and wife together whenever possible. Besides heading off potential dangers, seeing the husband and wife together is usually the most helpful for solving marriage problems, anyhow. Neither husband nor wife can exaggerate his side of the story or try to get away with outright lies when the other partner is right there to set the record straight. My husband has come to the conclusion that, although this is not always the case, usually it is a waste of time to see each partner separately, or one without the other. It is almost impossible to get anything but a distorted picture of what is really happening.

As for secretaries and other church personnel, they have also been known to present temptations to clergymen. One noted Christian executive and speaker says that he has had the same woman as secretary for a number of years. He warns that spending more hours a day with a secretary than with one's wife, as is the case with many executives, can lead to temptations. He heads these temptations off by adhering to some very strict rules. When the two of them are alone in the room, he *always* sees to it that the door is open. And he never, never drives her anywhere. He added, "If she were to break her leg, I would get someone else to bring her to the hospital." These seem to me to be good rules for one who wants to avoid even the appearance of evil.

Show Your Appreciation

Speaking from the wifely point of view let me add: please tell your wife how much you love her and appreciate her. And tell her often—at least daily. I saw a poster the other day which many of us could identify with. It said, "Do you love me or do you not—you told me once but I forgot." We forget very easily. Every person alive needs constant reassurance that someone loves him, and wives are no exception.

When you are specific about what you appreciate, it is even more helpful. Perhaps your wife went out of her way to run an errand for you. Or maybe dinner was exceptionally good. If she has a new hairdo or has lost some weight, please notice. And then tell her that you notice. Remember, even though you too are often under-appreciated, there are a number of ego-satisfactions built into your job. I know that you are working for the Lord and not for glory, but you do get a certain amount of notice. After all, you get up in front and have the entire congregation's attention at least once every week. And there are certain satisfactions in just being the pastor. Although your wife gets a little of the reflected glory, she does not get nearly as many "strokes." So she may be more dependent on you in this area than you are on her. Don't let her down.

Chapter 10

Words to Pastors' Wives

The Sheep-Dog Syndrome

Pastors' wives fall into two basic traps as they try to cope with their situations. The first of these is fitting into the stereotype of the minister's wife. These women are trying to be "good" ministers' wives. They want to do whatever is required of them. I suppose that a few of them are doing this because they feel coerced, but the majority of those whom I have met are very committed women. They are sincerely trying to do what God, their husbands, and the congregation want them to do. Unfortunately these three things are not always the same.

These women are working hard. My pastor brother once said that a minister's wife is in an awkward position. She's neither shepherd, like the pastor, nor is she really part of the flock. She's more like a sheep dog running around in circles with her tongue hanging out, panting from exhaustion.

She is probably caring for small children, keeping a spotless house, entertaining frequently, leading a women's study group, and singing in the choir. If someone else is in charge of a project which needs volunteers, the minister's wife's name heads the list. Further, if anyone else fails to fulfill an obligation, the minister's wife can be expected to step in.

Small wonder that many of these brave women begin to feel resentment and frustration, to say nothing of fatigue. They are working as hard as the pastor or any layman, yet they actually have the status of neither. It seems as if they have as many responsibilities as the pastor, but none of the privileges.

The pastor gets up in front and preaches on Sunday; he counsels people—sometimes even being instrumental in dramatically saving them from suicide or divorce; perhaps he is seeing people come to Christ as a result of his evangelistic efforts.

His wife, by contrast, tries to keep peace in the Ladies Aid, takes charge of the mid-week potlucks, and organizes the after-church coffee hour. He's doing all the exciting things, and she's stuck with the busy work.

They are both working in the church, but often their paths don't even cross during their working time for days at a stretch. They aren't really working together at all. They're simply both working for the same organization.

To those of you who find yourselves described above, I would say, "Stop." Take some time to carefully examine those activities you are involved in, and why.

If your gifts relate to these activities, you enjoy doing them, and your family is not suffering, go right ahead. You are one of a small minority who thrives on this type of schedule and probably would be unhappy if you curtailed your activities.

But for the majority of us who lack the gifts, the inclination, or the stamina to do all that seems required of us, carrying on as usual is not the answer.

The Cop-out

At the opposite end of the spectrum is the minister's wife who refuses to conform to the stereotype of a pastor's wife. She is a "cop-out." She involves herself as little as possible in the running of the church and often escapes the manse by taking an outside job. When questioned about life in the parsonage, her answer is predictable. It goes something like this: "My husband was called to the ministry, but I wasn't. I have my own life to live. I don't feel any special obligation as a pastor's wife."

This type of wife is often as frustrated as the sheep-dog type, although she pretends that everything is fine. I have talked to and listened to a number of these women. Sometimes the depth of their unhappiness can be measured by how intensely defensive they are about their life-style. They are unhappy because their husbands are (at least secretly) disappointed, the congregation feels cheated, and they themselves feel guilty.

Exercise Leadership Re Your Spiritual Gift

I believe there is a reasonable alternative. Neither being a sheep dog nor a cop-out is conducive to a successful ministry and a happy marriage.

Pastors' wives must accept their position of leadership. That is something that cannot be changed; it goes with the territory. I have had women tell me, "But I didn't know he was going to be a minister when I started going with him." Or, "I didn't have any idea of what being a pastor's wife would involve." To those women I always reply that God knew. If you really believe that He is in control and cares about you, then you must try to understand what are His purposes for you as a minister's wife.

Accepting the position of leadership, however, does not mean that you must do all the things that have traditionally been expected of you. It may mean doing some of them, although not because they are your job as a minister's wife.

How, then, do you figure out which things to do and which things to decline? As we have seen from Romans 12 and 1 Corinthians 12, each Christian has at least one spiritual gift. And he or she has the responsibility to develop and use that gift in his/her ministry. This is not only for ministers' wives, of course. Every Christian has a responsibility before God to use the gift or gifts which he has been given. So in that respect we are no different from any layman.

As ministers' wives our responsibility is to give leadership in the area of our special gift or gifts; then we must say a firm "No" to anything that does not fit in with this. For example, God has given me the gift of evangelism. He continues to use me to share my faith with others and lead them to Christ. Therefore my time and efforts should be directed not only toward excercising this gift but also toward helping others to do the same.

In addition to encouraging my own children in their witnessing and sharing with others, I continue to disciple other women in the area of evangelism. I also volunteer when anyone needs someone to teach a seminar or lead a class in evangelism. I accept invitations to speak at evangelistic coffees or teas and most any other gatherings that have to do with evangelism. I also spend time in visiting prospective church members with my husband and sometimes become quite involved in their problems. And when I am working with new Christians I often spend a lot of time with them in a one-to-one situation.

Music is another area in which I take responsibility since I have had many years of training and experience singing and playing both piano and organ. In each congregation which we have served I have played for services, along with the others who were capable. However, to enable others to use their talents as well, I have always been careful not to take over the music department. In our first two churches I gave free organ lessons to anyone who wanted to learn, who was willing to commit himself to play for services, and who had sufficient piano background to qualify. At times there were as many as seven students coming for weekly lessons.

Presently we are serving a mission church which has not yet bought an organ, so organ lessons have been curtailed for several years. I also play less frequently for Sunday services, since this congregation boasts a great many excellent musicians. I will probably never need to direct the choir here, since we have several people who are more experienced in conducting than I. At this point my contribution consists of taking my turn playing for the Sunday services, accompanying most of the soloists, and singing alto in the choir.

However consistently I may use my time in the areas of music and evangelism though, I just as consistently refuse to do other things which do not relate to these gifts. For instance, in all my years as a pastor's wife I have yet to teach a daily vacation Bible school class. I have on occasion taught Sunday school at various levels, but I do not consider it one of my primary responsibilities. I have not had a class for several years now. I also refuse to serve on those committees which do not relate to my particular abilities.

As all of you fellow ministers' wives know, this is not easy to do. I have not always succeeded, either. It is only in the last few years that I have gradually, with the help of my husband, come to these conclusions. If you are wondering whether you will be able to summon the courage to act on your convictions, let me add that *I still cannot refuse to do a certain job without feeling twinges of guilt.* No matter how busy I am at the time, no matter what my family responsibilities are at the moment, no matter how unrelated to my gifts the job may be, no matter how many others could do it just as well—I still feel guilty. Perhaps guilt, like leadership, also comes with the position. I hope that this will not always be the case. It certainly causes unnecessary emotional energy to be expended.

As psychologists point out, there are several kinds of guilt which we may feel. Among them is real guilt which results from doing something wrong. We are responsible to deal with this guilt.

There is a false guilt, however, which we ourselves or others may lay on us for something which is not really our responsibility at all. Some of this false guilt is put on us by members of the congregation who are still operating within their stereotyped image of the minister's wife. Much of it though we heap upon ourselves. We often imagine that we ought to be doing anything that is asked of us. The resulting guilt feelings are illegitimate and must be ignored.

With one or two outstanding gifts, it will be fairly simple for you to decide how to spend your time. However, many of you have a number of gifts. Often these have been uncovered and developed through years of ministry. Such gifts may include mercy, organization, teaching, and evangelism, for instance. If this is your situation, your guilt feelings may be intensified because you really are the person who can do a particular job better than anyone else in the congregation.

In this case the same advice which applies to pastors is relevant: get lay people involved. Select one or two key lay women in each area, and train them. Teach them what you know. This training is synonymous with discipling. Take them along on visitation, or teach a class together or chair a committee meeting jointly. Later have them initiate and lead activities while you support them by your presence and prayer.

At first you may be even busier than before. But soon the time invested will pay dividends. Eventually these women will begin to minister on their own. Then, when they are able to take on different jobs that you had previously been doing, you will be free to choose the areas in which your special ministry will be.

If you have several gifts but feel that you don't have the time to exercise all of them, how are you to choose? Personally, I would choose the one or two which are the closest to your husband's gifts. This enables the two of you to minister together as much as possible. For example, if your choice is between being chairman of a committee with which your husband is not involved or being on an evangelism team which he is leading, then my advice would be to choose the evangelism team.

Among the pastors and wives whom I interviewed, the happiest couples were those who worked together frequently. Ministering together seemed to add an extra dimension to their relationship that merely working together at another job would not provide. Not only were they helping and encouraging each other in their job, but they were also growing together spiritually. This is an added safeguard against one of you making strides in his or her faith and leaving the partner behind. Another side effect of ministering together in a certain area is that you will discuss your ministry together. This will also keep you from being left behind intellectually.

Keep Learning

Which brings us to the subject of the outgrown wife. Whether you have had a lot of formal education or just a little, you must keep learning in order to be an interesting person. A woman with a master's degree or a Ph.D. who has allowed her mind to go stale will not be as interesting to her husband as a woman who has never gone beyond high school but has an inquiring mind and uses it. If you read and are careful to listen to people who have something to say, you will remain interesting.

Your Dreams Must Be Portable

In chapter one of my book *The Creative Homemaker,* Bethany Fellowship, Inc., I have a couple of paragraphs which relate to being a wife. I quote—

"Someone once said that a wife should make her dreams portable. She must be ready to follow her husband wherever the Lord leads him. Many a man's career has been thwarted, his potential nipped in the bud, because his wife would not leave the geographical area in which she preferred to live. It seems particularly tragic when this happens to pastors, but ministers' wives are not immune to this temptation. I know of one minister who decided that God was leading him to serve a church out west. He accepted the call, only to meet an ultimatum from his wife. She was simply not moving. It was either the church or her. The man regretfully reversed his decision. This was one situation that came out into the open. Most go on behind the scenes. But it is an open secret among pastors that certain men are hamstrung in a choice of location because of their wives.

"It is not only pastors that God calls to relocate. There are many other men whose vocations demand that they move, often several times during their lives. Now I am not advocating more mobility for families. There are serious problems that accompany too frequent moves. *No* relocation of an entire family is accomplished without a certain amount of tension and anxiety. I am not trying to minimize this. . . . But a man should be free to find God's will for his life without having to fit it into a framework set up for him by his wife. He should not have to say, 'Lord, I'll go wherever you want, as long as it's not west of the Mississippi, because my wife won't live there.' "

Appearances Count

His wife's physical appearance is important to any man. No one prefers that his wife be excessively heavy, or dowdy, or unkempt. Some men appear not to care, but don't be fooled. The fact that your husband doesn't bring up the subject of your appearance does not mean that it doesn't matter to him. Any husband wants to be proud of his wife, and it is harder for him to be proud of you if you present an unattractive front to the world. You may have a wonderful mind and a beautiful soul which are the real "you." But your body is also part of you, and it's the part that people meet first. So don't let an unattractive appearance get in your way.

You do not want to look good only for your husband, of course. Your own self-respect suffers when you know that you look bad. As the mother of teenaged girls I know that whether a day is terrific or terrible can depend on how a hair-do turned out or whether one is carrying an extra five pounds or not. As we mature, we do not place such undue emphasis on these externals. But they are still an important part of our self-esteem.

Self-interest is involved, too. Your husband is meeting women all the time as part of his work. Some, of course, are not attractive to him. But many of the women that he is meeting in one capacity or another *are* very attractive, well-dressed, and carefully made-up. And occasionally he will encounter a woman who will deliberately set out to seduce him. I talked to an ex-pastor who told me that the woman for whom he left the ministry admitted that she had deliberately set out to get him. She knew he was a married man, but at their first counseling session she correctly assessed his marital dissatisfaction and his unmet needs. She immediately decided to try meeting those needs and succeeded in breaking up his marriage.

Marriages are not easily jeopardized by gaining a little weight or wearing clothes that are not particularly stylish. There are even cases of beautiful women losing their husbands to mousy little types. But nevertheless keeping up your looks is important.

One minister's wife whose husband is very handsome made a point of this in our interview. She is blessed with quite average looks, but she has always been careful to watch her figure and to dress as attractively as possible within her budget. Her husband is very devoted to her, and I don't think she worries about other women. But before I had asked anything about it, she mentioned the importance of watching one's looks. Many other women stressed this point. Some ex-wives said that one of the reasons their marriages had failed was that they had neglected their looks. So in case you are carrying more than ten or fifteen unnecessary pounds or in some other way have let your appearance slide, perhaps now is the time to do something about it.

Support Your Man

Every marriage partner needs help and encouragement from the other. And male egos being the fragile things they are, perhaps men in general need more support from their wives than the other way around. I am sure that this varies from one marriage to another. But one thing is sure: since society has begun questioning the traditional roles for husbands and wives, it has been increasingly more difficult for husbands to know just what their responsibilities are. As we women have begun to look at ourselves differently, our husbands have often become baffled. They love us and don't want to stand in the way of our fulfilling ourselves, so it has become harder and harder for them to know just how to lead. This makes it imperative for us to support them in their leadership.

Besides supporting your man in his role as husband, you can support him in his work. One of the important ways to do this is by exerting special care not to burden him with family or personal problems when he's about to leave for a board meeting, or just before he has to preach. Be especially careful not to start an argument at one of these times. That would hardly leave him in the proper frame of mind for delivering his sermon.

If at all possible, try to delay unloading your difficulties on him until he is feeling up. This is also the most advantageous time for you to present convincing arguments which in turn may enable him to make more understanding decisions.

During times of crisis in the church—if a group is questioning his leadership or there is a serious division in the congregation—you must of course give him extra, loving support. This is a time when he is especially vulnerable and needs to be told and shown that you believe in him totally.

Actually some of the more difficult traumas that husbands and wives face together are later discovered to be times of deepening love and growth in mutual respect. Paul says in Romans 5:3, 4 that "suffering produces endurance, and endurance produces character." James adds in chapter 1:3, 4, of his epistle that "the testing of your faith produces steadfastness." When the two of you are going through these troubles and depending on the Lord together, your relationship will be greatly enhanced. I can look back at some of the awful times we went through together and remember what a growing experience each of them was for our marriage. We didn't notice it at the time, of course. But from the perspective of a few years we can clearly see that that was the case.

In addition you can claim 2 Corinthians 1:4, "[God] comforts us in all our affliction, so that we may be able to comfort those who are in any affliction, with the comfort with which we ourselves are comforted by God." There is a reason for what we are going through. Soon after our most severe trial, my husband and I were able to help another couple who faced an experience similar to ours.

Another obvious way to support your man is by physical expressions of love. This is important to remember, because sometimes parsonage life can get so hectic that sex is squeezed out—it just kind of loses by default. You don't plan it that way; it just happens. This is a dangerous state of affairs.

Finding time for your sex life is actually easier than it seems. It merely requires a little imagination. If you find that you are always too tired at the end of the day or meetings keep you up too late, then bedtime is not going to work out for you. Simply face that fact and look for other times. If your husband comes home for lunch and your children don't, this could be a good time. Just be sure to lock the door and take the phone off the hook! Or you can arrange for other times during the day. After all, your husband plans his own schedule. If you ask him for a special time slot, I'm sure that he will be quite willing to cooperate.

Different times and places always add a special touch, anyhow. When the children are away you can bypass the bedroom for the downstairs sofa or someplace more interesting. There are many possibilities in your house, I am sure. Try them all. They can be your own little secret.

The Parsonage

Now a word about housekeeping. I am sure that somewhere there must be some pastors' wives who are terrible housekeepers, but I have personally never met them. And this is good, since an orderly house is important for creating a pleasant atmosphere for ourselves, our families and our guests. But don't succumb to a double standard for pastors' wives.

In our area we have occasional dust storms, and it seems that there is always some topsoil blowing around. I tell women to remember a motto I once saw describing how to cope with housekeeping in New York City: "Dust is an occupational hazard and cannot be considered my personal responsibility." I like that lighthearted approach. If you have small children, toys around are an occupational hazard. If you sew and have no sewing room which you can call your own, fabric spread out on the living room floor is now and then an occupational hazard.

After mentioning in my first book that my husband does not mind a "moderate amount of disarray," this has become a family joke. While I was finishing work on this book, our foster daughter moved in with us. This necessitated a lot of moving of furniture and clothes. It was almost like changing houses, since the contents of every closet and bureau drawer in the four bedrooms got sorted through and moved to a different location. At the same time we had two unrelated house guests. For a while my family teased me that the amount of disarray was rather immoderate. Of course one can't function effectively for long in the middle of disorder, but there are times when the only responsible thing to do is to give housekeeping a back seat temporarily. You may quote me on that!

Special Rewards

Besides the reward waiting in heaven for long-suffering pastors' wives, there are special benefits right here and now.

One of the benefits is a built-in acceptance in the church and community. You don't have to work to gain a place for yourself—it's already there by definition. When you move to a new location, the congregation and community are ready to accept you—sight unseen. You don't have to prove yourself or win their approval. All you have to do is receive the love and respect that are waiting for you.

Another reward is the positive side of the stereotype: you do get a chance to do everything that you're capable of doing and to be everything that you have the potential for being. You aren't likely to languish long with your talents either hidden or ignored. At some times in your frantic life you may fervently wish that none of your talents had ever been discovered. But in your heart of hearts you know that you are happier and more fulfilled by being able to use your gifts, even though you must put limits on their use.

A warning is appropriate however: don't try to run the church. Because of the ready-made acceptance and the over-abundance of opportunities to minister, you might be tempted to take over areas which are rightly none of your concern. A very small minority of pastors' wives seem to fall into this category. They gradually find themselves running, or trying to run, both the congregation and their husbands. If this is a temptation for you, let me say that not only will you eventually get a very bad reputation and lose the love of the congregation and possibly of your husband, but you will also ruin your husband's chances for calls. Your reputation will go ahead of you. No matter how highly people regard your husband, they will pass him over because they don't want to tangle with you. If the shoe fits . . .

Another reward which you should know, but perhaps take for granted, is that you are married to a godly man. Think of all of your friends or members of the congregation who are married to unbelievers: men who, no matter how decent they may be, cannot ever fully share their wives' goals and dreams. No two people can really walk together when they aren't going the same place. They can walk together for a little ways, but eventually their paths must diverge. You, on the other hand, have your husband's understanding, support, and direction. You can look to him for spiritual leadership and not be disappointed. Think for a minute of what it would be like to be married to a less spiritual man, and count your blessings.

Chapter 11

Words to Parents of PK's

Spend Time with Them

All children need their parents to spend time with them. It's not enough to see to it that they are fed, clothed, sent to school and to the dentist. They need evidence of their parents' love in time spent alone, just with them. Begin investing time in your children from the time they are very small. Then your relationship will grow and develop until finally you find that you need to spend even more time with them as they become teenagers. The dividends will be evident when they in turn initiate discussions with you, confiding the intricate details of their often agonizing problems.

One mother has observed that living with teenaged girls is moving from crisis to crisis. Those of you who have had teenaged girls know exactly what she means. At present we have three in that age bracket, including a foster daughter; so I can identify with that observation. I am glad to be able to spend time with them—I wouldn't miss those crises for anything.

Being sure that our children get enough of our time can present a problem for busy pastors and wives. You may have to block off certain segments of time for your children the way you reserve certain times for each other. We must remember that our children have the same needs as any other children, plus a few extra ones because of their position. They, too, are under pressure to conform to a certain stereotype. And it may be harder for them, being children, to understand the dynamics of the problem. As adults we at least know what motivates some of the people who make life difficult for us. Our children, on the other hand, may have no idea why they are being treated in a certain way. So they need our continued love and support. This means time spent with them. During their teenage years they are particularly vulnerable to feelings of resentment or even rebellion.

Perhaps you will want to have one night a week for family night. On this evening you might make popcorn and play Scrabble or just sit around and discuss whatever seems important at the moment. Although our family gave this idea a halfhearted try at one time, I must admit we were not successful with it. When we began family night our eldest, although only thirteen, was already in high school, so she had a lot of homework plus piano lessons and other activities. The younger ones also had commitments, and it was nearly impossible to find an evening which worked for everyone. Perhaps had we started it a few years earlier with a real commitment to the idea, it might have worked. Then again, it might not have succeeded. I do know, though, that it has worked successfully for a number of families.

Meal time has always been a family matter at our house. Before the first one started school we always had all three meals together. Then as they grew older and became involved in various activities, we had to adjust while still trying to meet our priorities. The high schoolers leave too early in the morning to have breakfast with us, but still we regularly have dinner together with family devotions immediately afterward. Sometimes one of the girls will have a school activity or a baby-sitting job which conflicts with our dinner hour, so she will not eat with us. But family meals are not missed arbitrarily.

Another way in which to spend quality time with children is to be there when they arrive home from school. I have always made this a priority. I can still remember how my own mother was always there after school, and how important it was to me. I would run in the house and call, "Mother!" She would answer, maybe from upstairs or the basement, "What do you want?" My answer was almost always the same: "Nothing." There was nothing specific that I needed or wanted to tell her. I just wanted to know that she was there. But then she would leave whatever she was doing and talk to me while I changed into my jeans to go outside and play. And all was right with my world. So I have made a commitment to do the same with my children.

Their father is usually at his study after school, too, and since this is only a few steps from the house, the girls often go over to talk to him about their day after they have greeted me. As they have matured and their own ministries have developed, they have wanted to go to him more and more for advice and encouragement. Unless he is in a very special conference with someone, he always drops what he is doing to talk to them.

Give Leadership as a Family

Your children, as PK's, are in the public eye along with the two of you. Your family is being scrutinized. This may not be fair, but it is a fact of life in the parsonage. So instead of viewing it as a hardship, you can encourage your children to look at it as an avenue of service. Your family can be a model for families in the congregation. If your children can see this as an opportunity for ministry, it can be a tremendously growing experience for them. If they realize that your family has something to offer, they will rise to the occasion.

But don't take your children for granted. Don't assume that they have the same concerns you do unless you have discussed these concerns with them. And whatever you do, don't burden them with the admonition to do a certain thing or refrain from doing it because of "what people will think." Some parents of PK's have told me that they have slipped into this sort of thing before they realized what they were doing. Think for a minute about how you chafe under that kind of phony restraint. And it's much harder for your kids. It may even be a major cause of rebellion. But this rebellion is unnecessary. Instead, share your ideas and desires for ministry openly and by example. Meanwhile God will develop sincere motivation within your child.

Give Them Your Values

Their ministry of course will also be dependent upon your ability to share your goals, and your success in imparting your value system. When your children share your values they won't be alienated from you. They will also accept your teaching and seek your advice, and this is what parenting is all about.

So often we let ourselves be influenced by the world's continual messages. "Be sure you let your child develop his own personality and go in the direction that is best for him; let him make up his own mind; whatever you do, don't push him, because then you will alienate him for sure; the generation gap is inevitable—we all have to learn to live with it."

After contending with this philosophy for a while, parents often feel guilty and apologetic. This twinge of guilt is misplaced. Certainly a child must and will develop his own individual personality, but it must not be without a great deal of help and guidance from you. That's exactly why God gave children parents. The familiar passages in Deuteronomy 6, Ephesians 6, several of the Proverbs, and many other scriptures make this very clear. I agree that from his earliest years your child must be encouraged to make responsible decisions for himself at whatever level of maturity he has achieved. But there are certain decisions which he cannot be allowed to make by himself. Among these are decisions relating to his spiritual welfare.

The state realizes that children cannot be allowed to choose whether or not they go to school. There is no question about it. Their welfare requires attendance. So they go. We as parents must be equally clear-headed and tough-minded about our children's spiritual welfare. When we carry out our parental responsibilities the way God intended, we and our children will have the same goals.

This saves our young people a lot of emotional turmoil. Just as they do not have to decide whether or not to get up and get dressed in the morning, they then do not have to waste time and energy asking, "Should I or should I not smoke pot, mess around with sex, or cheat on my tests?" They are then free to help us get on with the business of ministering to the world.

But just how do we transmit our values to our children? First of all, we must have a daily devotional life of our own. We must be in prayer and in the Word so that we are finding God's will for our own lives before we can help our children find His will in their lives. We cannot teach what we have not learned, or give what we do not have. We must never give them the idea that simply believing the gospel intellectually and being moral is the essence of the Christian life. Children sense any phoniness very quickly. We are not going to be able to foist on them a spirituality which we ourselves do not possess.

This is particularly important in discipline as our children become older. When they are young we know a lot more than they do and we are simply bigger than they. But as they become teenagers we need something more than our own say-so. When they are too big to spank, we need the authority that comes with an intimate knowledge of God's Word.

In this way we will be leading them into their own devotional life. My husband and I never specifically told any of our four children that they should have their own devotions. As soon as they were able to read adequately, they simply began. They had all seen that it was important to Dad and Mom, so it became important to them. I remember our youngest, at age three, long before she could read, going off into a corner with her picture Bible storybook. "Don't disturb me for a while," she ordered. "I'm going to have my quiet time."

Sharing spiritually with our children is another important aspect of taking our parental responsibility seriously. Our children have to know what is going on in our spiritual lives: our victories and our failures. They can become our prayer partners while they are still quite young. Obviously we will not tell them things which they are not equipped to handle. But there are a great many things which they can help us pray about. Sometimes they can even give us spiritual advice.

Give Them Spiritual Responsibility

Going a step further, I have come to see that it is not enough just to share spiritually with our children. They need to be part of the action. We must give them spiritual repsonsibility at a young age. In this way they become part of the solution instead of part of the problem. This is not only important for PK's, of course. It applies to all children of Christian parents. But it is especially important for us if we as families want to give direction to other families in our congregations.

We all know that we have to give our children responsibility in other areas. We teach them to work and hold part-time jobs; we let them handle money, care for younger children, and eventually drive cars. But while treating them as emerging adults in these areas, we often treat them as mere infants spiritually.

In addition to praying with us and for us, our children can be encouraged to share their faith with their friends, counsel them, and exhort them when necessary. They can also learn to accept those who are socially unacceptable. A minister's son of my acquaintance told how this is happening in his church group. One of the new Christians in the group is a young boy who is infuriatingly obnoxious much of the time. He evidently still has a lot to learn about the Christian life. The group as a whole has taken him on as a project. They show him that they love him, but they also correct him when necessary. The pastor's son and one girl, in particular, continue to give him some good, straight, biblical exhortation.

A girl in our teen group, who is now in college, stood out as a Christian in our local public high school. Her parents had always encouraged her to tell others about Christ. Students would come to her when they needed counsel or wanted to pray. This girl was able to lead several of her classmates to Christ.

Right now one of the English teachers, an outspoken non-Christian, has students from two of our church families. Both of these students have challenged him to consider Christianity. He shows no signs of softening, but he has admitted that he has a great deal of respect for these two young people.

Taking spiritual responsibility is a tremendous help for our children in their own personal walk of faith. When they are keeping their faces to the world—being always aware that they represent Christ to the world all around them—it gives them a built-in code of ethics. There is no way that they are going to get drunk, or shoplift, or join other escapades in which their friends engage when they realize that they, personally, are Christ's representatives to their friends. They become wonderfully inner-directed. This enables them to resist peer pressure. It is then not a matter of doing what you, their parents, want. It's a matter of doing what God wants.

Then we together, parents and children, are trying to find God's will. When our children learn to minister alongside of us, they will find out that they are making great strides spiritually, and they will not have as much reason to resent their position. They will be reaping the rewards of ministry along with us. This is the best gift we could possibly give them.

Chapter 12

Words to Congregations

Don't Add to Your Pastor's Job

The average pastor grapples with a tremendously large job description and unfair expectations, always trying to stretch his twenty-four-hour day as far as possible. It is up to you, the members of his congregation, to do something about his problems. Your pastor is not going to complain since he pretty much knew what he was getting into before he started. He will probably just keep on trying to do the best he can, at the same time feeling he spends insufficient time on too many things and so does nothing thoroughly.

In order to be really effective—to be the kind of preacher and pastor which he can be and which you want him to be—he needs your help. There are specific steps which you can take. There may be others also, but these suggestions are gleaned from my own nineteen years in the parsonage, from much reading on the subject, and from interviews with pastors and wives from many different denominations across the country.

The first suggestion deals with telephoning the pastor. Before you phone him at all, please ask yourself whether someone else might be able to answer your question just as well. If so, phone that person. Most laymen don't mind taking an occasional call at work. And of course, neither does the pastor. But people quickly forget that the pastor also has *his* work. And when only a few people make unnecessary calls to the pastor his valuable time is quickly consumed.

By the way, we pastors' wives get a lot of unnecessary phone calls, too. Don't forget, our time is also valuable. I must confess to having feelings of resentment when someone regularly calls me about something unimportant and begins by saying, "I didn't want to bother the pastor, so I called you." We are not exactly lollygagging around, ourselves.

While I am on the subject of calls, I'd like to add something else which many wives mentioned. Please try the study or office number first when you are trying to reach the pastor. He does spend most of his working hours there except for the times that he is out making calls or attending meetings somewhere else. If you can't reach him there, at least you will not be disturbing anyone else, except possibly the secretary. And answering the phone is part of her job. If you try the house first, you will disturb his wife.

If the pastor is not home, please resist the temptation to tell his wife all the details of the problem that you need to talk to the pastor about. She almost certainly will not be able to help you anyway, so there is no reason to take up her time. Contrary to popular belief, she probably does not know what the carpet order for the nursery was, or the names of all the members on a particular committee, or what the pastor wanted to talk to Mrs. Jones about. She will try not to be rude to you, but you really are wasting her time by asking.

I'm telling you this since I'm sure that most members of congregations have no idea of how much of our time is taken up in this way. A word to the wise . . .

If no one else can take care of your problem except the pastor, please try to be considerate about timing your call. Unless it is a genuine emergency, I consider it quite thoughtless to disturb the pastor anytime on Sunday or during the dinner hour on weekdays. Sundays are very exhausting days for him, and he needs whatever rest he can sneak in. And the dinner hour is an important family time. Sometimes we take our phone off the hook during dinner and devotions, but I don't really like to do that. I always think that there might be a real emergency, and there's also the problem of possibly forgetting to replace the receiver after dinner.

There are probably other specific times when your pastor is studying and does not want to be disturbed. Ask him when these times are and honor them. One of our pastor friends does not want to take any calls between 8:00 a.m. and 10:30 a.m. on any day. That is his special studying time. For those preachers who must prepare two sermons every week, it is likely that Saturday is a day during which they will not want any interruptions. My husband is one of these men. If someone visits him for an hour on Saturday, that almost certainly means that he gets to bed an hour later that night. If there is something special that he wants to attend on Saturday evening, he plans ahead, of course. But even if he writes his sermons earlier in the week, he prefers to review them on Saturday. If your pastor also uses his Saturdays for sermon preparation, please try not to bother him then.

Another question which you should ask yourself if you are regularly phoning or visiting your pastor or asking him to visit you is: Am I taking a disproportionate share of his time? Your problem may seem terribly important to you, but have you stopped to think that the congregation and church community is full of people with problems? If each one took as much of the pastor's time as you do, would he have any time left for anything else? Sometimes that is exactly the situation. So many people are putting demands on his time that his preaching and his family life are suffering.

Also, respect your pastor's time off. Although I realize that many others put in long hours at their jobs and sometimes even take work home, I daresay that none of you regularly works seven days a week. If your pastor takes Monday or some other day of the week off, please don't call him on that day unless it really is an emergency. After all, even if he takes one day off, he is still working six. Most pastors work a great many—if not most—evenings, also.

Encourage Him

On the positive side, there are some other things which you can do to help your pastor. Praying for him is of primary importance. You have heard this many times before; nevertheless, it is worth repeating. He is in a position of special spiritual responsibility, so the devil is going to give him special attention. Your pastor may appear spiritually strong to you; possibly he does have spiritual reserves which are greater than those which most of us possess. But that is exactly why the devil is going to concentrate his best efforts on him. After all, when a person is not going anywhere or doing anything for the Lord, he is of no particular interest to the devil, either.

And the devil especially wants to break up families, because that is the way to undermine a whole culture and bring it to ruin. Obviously the marriages of spiritual leaders would be prime targets. So pray for your pastor in relation to his wife and family in addition to

134

praying for him in his work. Now that we have seen some of the real and specific problems which he and his family face, perhaps you will be able to pray for them with more feeling and intensity.

Another way to encourage your pastor is verbally. You may think that he realizes how much you appreciate him. But sometimes he has no way of knowing unless you tell him. Often a pastor doesn't really know how much people care until he decides to take a call somewhere else. Then many of the people, genuinely distressed by his leaving, begin to tell him how much they appreciate him and how they wish he wouldn't leave. Things might be quite different in many churches if all the laymen who really love their pastor would tell him so.

The October, 1978, issue of *Pulpit Helps* contains a piece entitled "Praise Your Pastor." It says, "When was the last time you complimented your pastor? Praise, when timely and sincere, has the power to transform discouraged persons into happy, radiant individuals. A recent study reported by the Journal of Educational Psychology demonstrated that persons receiving praise became more effective and accomplished even greater tasks than those who were ignored and reproved. . . . As one writer said, 'To make his abilities apparent to the other is to help him know himself as he really is.' Praise is always an incentive to any pastor to accomplish, to achieve, to excel. If you want his sermons to improve, make sure you let him know when he does a good job. . . . When we praise, we give a spiritual boost to our fellow-man." I couldn't agree more. We all work better when we are lovingly challenged to outdo ourselves.

Hebrews 13:7 says, "Obey your leaders and submit to them; for they are keeping watch over your souls, as men who will have to give account." This is saying that some day your pastor is going to be held accountable for you. When you realize what that means, you will try your best to help him in any way that you can.

Ministry Is Your Business, Too

As people of God we must come to the realization—intellectually and on a gut level—that ministry is the responsibility of every Christian. The early church knew that. They didn't expect their pastors to do the work for them. In some cases they didn't even have a pastor until the congregation was well established.

This was the case with the Antioch church. The story is told in Acts 11:19-26. Some Jewish Christians settled there because of the persecution after Stephen's death. They shared their faith with their new friends and neighbors in Antioch. "And the hand of the Lord was with them, and a great number that believed turned to the Lord." When the church in Jerusalem heard how the Antioch church was growing, they decided that the Antioch group needed a pastor, so they sent Barnabas.

The pastor does have a leader's share of responsibility. That doesn't leave you off the hook, however, since everyone should aspire to spiritual leadership.

In "The Urgency of the Equipping Ministry" Paul Benjamin writes, "To solve the problem of the overloaded minister, some congregations move into a multiple-staff situation. Yet . . . this route is inadequate if the equipping-ministry concept is absent. In fact, adding more staff only makes it easier for a congregation to sit back while they pay others to minister for them. It often perpetuates the whole non-equipping system." The answer, Benjamin effectively argues, is for each staff member to be "following the equipping-ministry concept. Whether a person serves in education, in music, in clerical work, in counseling, or in evangelism, one of the primary responsibilities of that area of service is to equip others. . . . Fundamental to our thinking must be the radical idea presented in the New Testament—every Christian is a minister of Jesus Christ." [19]

Findley B. Edge in his exciting book *The Greening of the Church* minces no words in his section on the call of the church to mission. He talks about how the Pharisees of Jesus' day had misunderstood God's call. "They thought God had called them to be a *separated people* rather than *a people on mission*. The danger the churches face today is exactly this same misunderstanding. . . . We must understand with clarity [that] the 'new' Israel is called for precisely the same purpose as was the original Israel . . . our call is a call to a task. . . . *We are called to a mission*. God is not calling us simply to give us something. . . . His dealing with the first Israel should stand as a blazing warning as to what happens to a people who fail to understand and fulfill the purpose of his call." And to give further emphasis to these strong words he adds, "The primary responsibility for God's ministry in the world is the responsibility of the laity and not the clergy . . . we have been relying upon the wrong people to do the work of the ministry. God has called his people to be his ministers. His people must understand, accept, become equipped for, and fulfill this call." [20]

Once we digest this concept and make it part of our lives, a tremendous burden will lift from the shoulders of all of our over-worked pastors. Each pastor will then become the leader of a great team of ministers. He is chosen as the captain, but every church member is part of the team.

The Wages of Ministry

Another way in which you can encourage your pastor is simply by paying him a salary that is adequate for his needs. First Timothy 5:17, 18 reads, "Let the elders who rule well be considered worthy of double honor, especially those who labor in preaching and teaching; for the scripture says . . . 'The laborer deserves his wages.' "

We are all tempted to think that we need more than we do. Yesterday's luxuries so quickly become today's needs. Our homes are full of appliances and gadgets which are not necessary, and as Ronald Sider has pointed out in his excellent book *Rich Christians in an Age of Hunger*, probably no one reading this book would actually need to buy any more clothes for at least two years. We all own enough warm clothes to take care of our physical needs. We buy new ones because the old ones are out of style or simply because we want new ones. We also do not need television sets, or restaurant meals, or hairdressers, or recreational vehicles, or steak for dinner occasionally.

Another excellent book dealing with the necessity to pay attention to preserving our resources if we wish to avert disaster is *The Closing Circle* by Barry Commoner. The entire evangelical community has been guilty on this score right along with non-Christians. Too often there has not been a conspicuous contrast between us and the world in our handling of the earth's resources and the money which God has given us.

But having said that, I will quickly add that there is no reason, biblical or otherwise, why pastors should be forced to sacrifice more in this area than anyone else. They should, as spiritual leaders, be an example with their life-styles, as should all mature Christians. But their standard of living should be their own choice before God just as any layman's is. If your pastor is forced into a lower standard of living than his parishioners because his income is less than theirs, you are robbing him of the joy of giving. He is then not giving leadership by living on a smaller percentage of his income and giving the rest to the church and the poor. He is not an example for anyone to follow. He is simply forced to live the way he does.

A pastor should be paid according to the level of income of the congregation he serves. There is probably no reason why a pastor should have an income which is greater than that of the average of his parishioners (unless possibly he has tremendous medical bills or other special needs). But by the same token I can see no reason why a pastor should be paid less than the average income of the members of the congregation.

After all, the congregation is his social group. You are putting him in an embarrassing position if he is not able to participate in activities in which most of the others in the congregation are involved. He doesn't want to say that he can't afford to attend a certain retreat or outing. And if there are breakfast and lunch meetings in restaurants, which seems to be a trend today, your pastor certainly wants to be able to pick up his own check. He will probably appreciate someone else's getting the tab occasionally, but he does not want to feel patronized.

Unless your congregation is made up exclusively of doctors, college professors, and lawyers, the pastor has considerably more education than the average layman in your church. He may be paying off his loans for his schooling for many years after he enters the ministry. I have even encountered some pastors who were paying off college and seminary debts until a few years before they retired. I would hope that this sort of thing is not happening anymore.

Your pastor also has some special expenses which most of you do not have, such as the continuing need to subscribe to periodicals and buy books. In order to do a good job of sermon preparation, a preacher needs a fairly large library. For a start he needs several sets of commentaries and an encyclopedia, plus a large number of books on a variety of subjects in theology. And there is no point at which his library is complete. Books are continually being written, both in theology and current problems. He needs these books.

There is also the matter of continuing education. Today there are a great many seminars and conferences available to the pastor which deal with church growth, counseling, evangelism, time management, and other subjects which can be helpful to him in his work. Although he may feel that attending one of these seminars occasionally would be helpful to his ministry, he is usually not in a position to pay for it himself.

Business firms regularly pay to send their executives and other key employees to training sessions. It is as necessary for pastors to keep fresh and up-to-date as for business executives; their jobs are surely no less important. Shouldn't the church's business be conducted as efficiently and well as industry's? And shouldn't we be willing to pay for this?

In line with this it is probably good for us to remember that the church is our first area of responsibility for giving. In *They Cry Too!* Lucille Lavender makes a timely point: "Though many people do give generously, the church is suffering because it is not receiving its rightful share. Much of the giving done by its members goes to many agencies outside the church . . . church members should always regard their church as their first responsibility. That is the organization that utilizes it in the most productive way possible. What does not occur to people . . . is that *without the church all of these other organizations would not and could not exist.* Because of the church they came into being, and because of the support of the church they continue to exist. Probably as high as 95 percent of outside agencies' support comes from people who belong to churches." [21] If we are taking our financial responsibility to the church seriously, we will have no trouble paying our pastors appropriately.

His Wife

Now that you have seen some of the pressures which influence the pastor's wife, you can contribute toward easing them. The pastor's wife can try to eliminate duties not in line with her gifts and she can better organize her time, but if you as a congregation don't change your ways, she will probably never get rid of her feelings of guilt.

When you refuse an office in the local PTA or plead that you are too busy to collect for the muscular dystrophy society, you may feel guilty, too. But that is nothing compared to the guilt your pastor's wife feels when she refuses to do a particular task in the church. Turning down the PTA is turning down men; refusing the church is refusing God. That isn't exactly the case, of course. The job in the church which she has refused may be less important to the Lord than the PTA job, and your pastor's wife may not be the person to do it, at all. Probably she should never have been asked. But she still has to live with the ubiquitous, nagging feeling that she is somehow hindering the Lord's work. That isn't a very nice feeling to live with, believe me—nor is it mentally healthy.

Perhaps you are also asked sometimes to do things in the church which you must refuse. As a result you feel guilty. If this is the case, then you can better understand your pastor's wife's problem.

However, there are two basic differences between your situations. First of all, you almost certainly don't get asked to do things as often as she does, nor are you living in the pressure cooker atmosphere of the parsonage at the same time. Secondly, and this is the most important difference, you do not have the same emotional involvement with the church that your pastor's wife does. Even if you are the number one lay man or woman in the church, it is not the same. You see, if things do not go well in the church, *your* husband will not lose his job.

Think about that. That's exactly the pressure your pastor and his wife can never escape, even though they may not be consciously thinking about it. Even when things are going exceptionally well, some little incident will bring this thought to the surface. No, of course you wouldn't fire your pastor. (Or would you?) But the board can make it very clear that it would be best for him to look elsewhere. And then your pastor's wife will wonder how much of the fault is hers. So please do all you can to keep from adding to her guilt feelings.

One woman who has spent many years in the parsonage and whose husband is presently in business said that she has enjoyed comparing life inside the parsonage and out. She insists that she can actually do more in the church now since she's not the pastor's wife, because she's out from under the pressure.

Her comments were given to a group of pastors' wives as we were discussing our role. The immediate question at hand was whether or not we should be the first to volunteer to bring casseroles, etc., for various church functions. This woman was quite vehement as she declared that we should be the last to be asked to volunteer for things like that, because we're making such a contribution just by coping with all the difficulties of parsonage living.

The rest of us were in no position to compare life in the parsonage with life as laymen, since our adult lives were spent as pastors' wives. But it gave us something to think about. In any case, let your pastor's wife figure out where the Lord wants her to use her gifts— she will have plenty of opportunities.

A way in which your pastor's wife may choose to cope with some of the pressures of parsonage living is to spend time with a special friend. If she does choose a friend from the congregation, and that friend isn't you, don't resent whoever it is. The woman she chooses may be closer to her age, or her temperament, or in some other way meet her special needs. This in no way reflects upon you. One person can't be "best friends" with everyone.

On the positive side, there are things that you can do to help your pastor's wife. When you send her husband off to a retreat or a seminar, pay her way, too. Most of these meetings are no longer planned for men only, and she will probably benefit as much as he. You will be enabling them to have some much-needed time together. Just as important, they will be adding another dimension to their relationship as they learn together.

Every once in a while one of the women in the congregation will invite me out to a nice restaurant for lunch—for my birthday or some other occasion—just to show her appreciation. Or sometimes one will send me a valentine or give me a little gift. These gestures mean a lot to me. I'm not a very sentimental person, but I am always touched by these tangible evidences that people care. I am sure that other pastors' wives are equally appreciative of this sort of thing.

As in the case of your pastor, the simplest and perhaps most neglected way of showing your appreciation to his wife is by your words. When a man makes a point of thanking me for the hours of practice which he knows are required behind the scenes in order to play a difficult accompaniment for a solo, or a woman tells me that she appreciates the fact that I always look nice, or an elder thanks me for doing something I had thought no one noticed, it makes my whole week.

About the Parsonage

Since a good percentage of pastors' families still live in parsonages and probably will for some time to come, it is a subject that needs discussing.

The pastor's house, like his salary, should be of the size and quality of those of most of his parishioners. The denomination to which I belong—the Christian Reformed Church—has always been very responsible about this. In fact, often the parsonage is one of the nicest houses in the community. This is a real credit to our people. Our home mission board is also generous in this regard.

Others are not so fortunate. I have heard some terrible tales about inadequate parsonages. Please see to it that your parsonage is not one of them. Pastors and their families are in a tough enough situation without having to live in cramped quarters, or put up with pipes that leak, furnaces that don't work properly, or what have you.

As far as the maintenance of the house is concerned, I have a suggestion to make which, if acted upon, could make life easier for all of us. I would like to see each congregation have a special parsonage committee—this could probably consist of a couple of members of the building and grounds committee—who would come through the house twice a year (by advance appointment at the wife's convenience!) and confer with the pastor and his wife about necessary repairs and painting. Perhaps it would not always be possible to make all the desired improvements immediately, but in that case they could be planned for some future time. At least the family would know where they stood. This plan would save the embarrassment of having to come begging every time the screen door breaks, or a faucet leaks, or the carpet needs replacing. The committee would see for themselves, with a minimum of effort, what needs to be done. A twice-yearly visit would not be much of a bother, and you would be helping your pastor and his wife more than you can probably realize.

Another thing to keep in mind about the parsonage is that, although it belongs to the church, it is the pastor's home as much as if he owned or rented it. It is not an extension of the church to be used whenever space is needed. Please don't ask to use the basement, or family room, or whatever for a Sunday school class or a vacation Bible school class. If the congregation has outgrown its facilities, it needs to build or make some other arrangements. The parsonage is the pastor's home. Period. When landlords rent out houses they do not expect to use certain rooms at certain times simply because they own the building. Neither should the church.

A psychologist who has also been a pastor and who has counseled a great many pastors and their wives over the years is quite outspoken about telling congregations to keep hands off the parsonage. He believes that this abuse of the pastor's house has been a factor in the precarious mental health of many wives.

Many of the complaints that I heard about living in parsonages would be eliminated or at least greatly reduced if the pastor's house were not next door to the church. When the parsonage is not so accessible there is much less running in to borrow things, fewer requests to use rooms, and a greater sense of personal privacy for the entire family. Women who have lived in both situations say they much prefer being in the neighborhood of the church, but not right next door. A few blocks away is ideal.

Our family has had both experiences, and I heartily agree that a little distance does wonders. I think it is important to live in the neighborhood, particularly if you as a congregation are trying to reach your community. It doesn't make sense to me for the pastor to live several miles from the church if he is going to lead the way in inviting his neighbors to church. I don't see how one can have an effective ministry if he doesn't live with the people he's trying to minister to.

But that doesn't mean that the parsonage has to be adjacent to the church. There are some real advantages for ministry in being part of a neighborhood, as several women pointed out to me. Sometimes when you are right next to the church, you tend to be excluded from the neighborhood. Our present situation is similar to this. The church is on one side of the parsonage, vacant lots are behind, and a school is across the street. We find ourselves on the edge of a neighborhood instead of part of it.

In our previous congregation the parsonage was right in the middle of a real neighborhood, a few blocks from the church. We were very much involved with all of our neighbors. We found it to be an ideal situation both for our family and for our evangelistic efforts.

Except for the initial time saved by being able to buy one piece of land and build both the church and parsonage on it, I see few advantages in having the parsonage next door to the church. One pastor told me that he kind of liked the convenience of being able to run next door from his study at the church whenever he liked, but he conceded that he would probably get more done if he didn't take so many breaks. And he would be very willing to give this up in order to gain a more normal living situation for his family.

So is you are planning to build or buy a house for your pastor's family, please talk this over with them before you proceed.

Leave His Kids Alone

When talking to pastors and their wives about their children, I stress the opportunity for our families to give leadership by example. My husband and I challenge our children to take advantage of their position to serve the Lord in a special way. I tell them this because the double standard exists: they are in the limelight. Therefore they might as well use the situation for good.

That does not mean that I believe the existing double standard is right or fair. So I am telling you, as congregations, to realize that PK's are children like any other children. They may have some spiritual advantages that other children do not have. (But if you grant that, it is not a very good reflection on you as parents, is it?) However, they also have special pressures built into their life in the parsonage. So don't demand anything of them that you wouldn't demand of your own children.

This particularly applies to Sunday school teachers and youth leaders. Please treat the pastor's children exactly the same as any others. Don't expect them to know more, or behave better. And please, if a PK and another child are disrupting a class or in some other way causing a problem, don't reprimand the PK more strongly than the other child.

I know what your subconscious motivation for this kind of treatment can be. You realize that if you anger the PK, he will almost surely return anyway: he has to come. The other child's commitment to the group may be a lot more tenuous. If he is a community contact, he will return only if he likes the group and the leader. Even if his parents are church members, they may not force him to attend the youth group. So you tend to court the other children and take the PK's for granted. But please think about the unfairness of this treatment and honestly try to discover whether or not you have been guilty of it so that you can remedy the situation.

If all congregations were to act on the suggestions made in this chapter, we would see a wonderfully transformed clergy and their families! I guarantee that you will not regret whatever steps you take toward understanding and helping your pastor and his family. You will receive the rewards of a renewed relationship; you will also be a better person for having truly helped another.

Chapter 13

"But Be Transformed"

Our calling in life as Christians is to live a special kind of life. Paul says in the first part of Romans 12, "Present your bodies as a living sacrifice, holy and acceptable to God. . . . Do not be conformed to this world *but be transformed* by the renewal of your mind, that you may prove what is the will of God, what is good and acceptable and perfect." Being conformed is, of course, much easier than being transformed. Drifting downstream with the culture takes no effort at all; fighting the current to go upstream requires hard work. And it is constant work: the minute we relax our efforts we fall back with the mainstream of the world again.

The Lord calls us to self-denial and sacrifice; the world tells us to coddle ourselves. Nowhere is this tension more obvious today than in the area of marriage. The world says that love is feeling good about each other, love is happiness; the Lord says in 1 Corinthians 13 that love is enduring: hanging in there, no matter what comes. Whether or not we feel good at a particular time is not the issue. Our job is to see to it that the work of the kingdom is accomplished. Personal happiness may never be our goal.

Too often the church takes on the style of the community instead of influencing the community. For instance, in areas where the community is rascist, the church has often been rascist. The American church in general has shown little more concern for the poor than has the world. Where the community has made financial success its goal, the church has often followed suit. Someone has said that the church is going in the same direction as the world—it

simply takes a little longer to get there. This takes about a generation.

We must admit, to our shame, that this has been the case with
divorce. When I was a small child living in a conservative community, the only divorces I knew about were those of Hollywood
movie stars. Then divorce became acceptable to the culture around
us, and many non-Christians started ending their marriages. But
still the church in general would not accept divorce among its
members. Now, a generation later, although the church is not entirely comfortable with divorce, it is more and more giving its approval.

There are a number of books on the market today written by
evangelical Christians which talk about the right to remarry and
build a new life after divorce. Some of these books talk in such
glowing terms that one is left with the impression that perhaps life
after divorce is more exciting and satisfying than the lives of
monogamous couples. The inference is that going through the
problems and struggles of divorce and remarriage is such a growing
experience that by staying married the rest of us are missing out.

Singles groups in some congregations are made up almost exclusively of divorced people. And now the clergy are beginning to join
the ranks of divorced church members. We are simply following the
world's direction.

Now of course there must be forgiveness and acceptance in the
church for divorced people as well as for any other repentant sin-
ners. I don't want to minimize this in any way. But in order to receive forgiveness there must be an acknowledgment of sin.

Counselors of Pastors and Wives

This is where the role of Christian psychiatrists, psychologists,
and others who counsel pastors and their wives is crucial. In any
marriage counseling it is important that you who are in the position
of giving advice—whether direct or indirect advice—are sure that
you are giving the word from the Lord. Even when you help the
person lay out different options for himself and tell him that he
must make a choice, you are giving advice by your approval of the
options. If divorce is one of the options you are helping the person
to consider, then you have given your blessing to the divorce. And
you must take responsibility for giving this kind of guidance.

Although Christians know that divorce is sin, often Christian counselors seem not to keep this foremost in their minds. Recently a young bride came to me in tears about the advice she had gotten from her pastor who had married her some months previously. He told her that God's first plan was obviously for her to remain married to her husband. But since they were having problems, the pastor said that perhaps God had another plan which would be for her to divorce her husband and marry someone else who would be a better husband. This young woman was quite upset by the casual attitude the pastor had toward the marriage at which he had officiated. No mention was made of the sin of breaking a marriage. I am sure that she then came to me knowing that I would tell her to stick with her marriage and try to work out the problems. Several ex-pastors' wives whom I interviewed also said that Christian counselors had advised them to divorce their husbands.

Jesus says in John 15:7 that if we are abiding in His will, we can ask anything and it will be done for us. We know that the healing of a marriage is always in God's will. We aren't always that sure in a particular case that physical healing is in His will. We know that each person has a time to die. Sometimes when we are praying for physical healing, we don't know whether this healing is God's will or not. But it is never God's will that a marriage be broken.

Let's take a look again at what the Scripture says about marriage and divorce. In Matthew 19:6-8 Jesus says that in marriage a man and woman are "no longer two but one flesh. What therefore God has joined together let not man put asunder. . . . For your hardness of heart Moses allowed you to divorce your wives, but from the beginning it was not so. And I say to you: whoever divorces his wife except for unchastity, and marries another, commits adultery." Romans 7:2, 3 reads, "A married woman is bound by law to her husband as long as he lives. . . . Accordingly, she will be called an adulteress if she lives with another man while her husband is alive." In 1 Corinthians 7 Paul continues, "To the married I give charge, not I but the Lord, that the wife should not separate from her husband (but if she does, let her remain single or else be reconciled to her husband)—and that the husband should not divorce his wife."

These passages are pretty straightforward. I don't think we have any trouble seeing what they are saying. Our trouble comes in trying to live by them. Our tendency is always to be conformed to the culture instead of being tranformed. But in *The Incendiary Fellowship* Elton Trueblood makes the point that Christians are in trouble whenever they stop being in tension with the current mentality of the culture around them. And since the coming of the Holy Spirit we do have the power available to live this renewed life. This applies to our marriages as well as to anything else.

Even serious, evangelical scholars whose biblical exegesis is sound on every other point tend to compromise on the subject of divorce. Dwight Hervey Small, writing on divorce and remarriage in the Fuller Seminary magazine, says: "Divorce and remarriage is a disruption, technically sinful in view of God's pure, creative intent," and then he goes on to say that the divorced person can repent and then "exercise the grace that permits [God's] blessing upon a new marriage." [22] To say that divorce and remarriage are a "a disruption [which is] technically sinful" is theological doubletalk. Sin is sin. There is no such thing as a technical sin.

We tend to shy away from calling sin by its rightful name today. Sometimes we write it off as sickness. Just think of how often when talking about a person who has committed a grisly murder or some other atrocity the comment will be made, "He must be sick." No one says, "What a terrible sinner." People might talk about the awful crime, but they seldom talk about its being a sin against God.

We don't like to think of divorce as being a sin against God either, but the Bible clearly states that fact. Whether or not something is a sin isn't determined by what we think about it, but by whether or not it agrees with God's will. And we find God's will from the Scriptures. In *No Little People* Francis Schaeffer talks about the prophet Nathan's commentary on David's sin with Bathsheba. He delivered God's words in 2 Samuel 12:10, "Now therefore the sword shall never depart from thine house; because thou hast despised me." In despising the commandment of the Lord, David had despised the Lord himself. There is no difference: To despise one is to despise the other." [23]

So knowing that it is God's will that marriages be healed, reconciliation must always be the aim. This may take months, or perhaps even years. Temporary separation may be necessary in certain cases. But in counseling pastors and their wives, reconciliation must always be the goal. It appears that this is not the case with many Christian counselors today. Several of the divorced pastors and wives with whom I talked said that they felt betrayed when their spouses were counseled to get a divorce.

In one case the couple had dated for several years before marriage and had been married for twenty years. They had four children. There was no third person involved—no problems which seemed so serious to the husband that they could not have been worked out. But his unhappy wife was advised by a Christian counselor (who had never met with her husband) to get a divorce. Now they are both unhappy and it appears that his effectiveness as a pastor has been destroyed.

In another case a pastor's wife was having problems relating to stresses in the parsonage, so she and her husband sought out a Christian counselor for her. Instead of helping her to deal with her situation, the counselor helped her to run away from her problems. He became romantically involved with her. They subsequently broke up both of their marriages (which involved several children) to marry each other. The woman's ex-husband was stunned. He could hardly believe what was happening. He is now understandably bitter about Christian counselors.

Too often counselors have peace, harmony, or a good relationship as the ultimate goal in marriage counseling. These are all worthy goals, but they aren't enough. The Bible demands that reconciliation be the ultimate aim, and it promises the power to move toward it. When a counselor has the wrong final goal he will end with an unbiblical solution. We cannot expect to get beyond that at which we aim.

Marriage More Than Relationship

There is a mistaken idea abroad today that marriage is synonymous with a relationship between a man and a woman. By this thinking when the relationship is going well, the marriage is viable. However, if the relationship comes upon bad times, the marriage is said to be dying; and if the relationship is seriously broken, the marriage is pronounced dead. At this point divorce is seen as the only option. After all, if the marriage is dead, the only logical next step is to hold the funeral.

I have heard individuals say that because their marriage relationship was never what it should have been, they never had a marriage. In one case a pastor who had been married for over twenty years and had four children claimed that he'd never really had a marriage. A sad but interesting aspect to this case is that the wife who had worked side by side with her pastor husband for all of those years thought that they had a good relationship. Whether or not a relationship is what it should be is obviously very subjectively determined. The conclusion which is reached depends upon who is making the judgment and on what basis.

God doesn't see marriage that way. Certainly marriage is a relationship between two people. But it is much more. Fundamentally, basically, it is a commitment: a commitment which two people make to each other, before God, to take on the responsibilities of their becoming one flesh. The commitment is not even to become one; God has made them one by the act of marriage. The commitment is simply to live together and love each other until death *because they are one flesh*. When two people are working at marriage, when they are loving each other the way God defines love in the well-known 1 Corinthians 13 passage (being patient and kind, not insisting on one's own way, not being resentful, enduring everything), they will have a beautiful relationship.

If one or both partners fail to do this, the relationship may turn sour. But this does not mean that the marriage is dead or even dying. A marriage is an objective entity which exists before God as long as both partners live. Man can deliberately break a marriage, just as he can break any of God's laws. But a marriage does not die any more than God's laws die. We must understand this clearly. To say that a marriage has died is to absolve the partners of responsibility. But God holds us responsible. We are able to break our marriages, but we must realize that we are sinning when we do so.

God has spoken very clearly on this point. We hear only "let not man put asunder." Not a word about exceptions for those who are experiencing serious difficulties in their relationships. Nowhere does the Scripture say, "If you've tried to make a go of it for several years, and things just seem to be getting worse, you are free to divorce. After all, I'm a loving God and I don't want you to suffer."

Nor does God say, "If you are fighting all the time, it's better for the children that you divorce." One often hears that divorce is the lesser of two evils. Those who say this are really saying that they have a choice between two sins: to keep on fighting or to divorce. But God does not operate that way. The choice He gives us is between sinning and not sinning. First Corinthians 10:13 reads, "God is faithful, and he will not let you be tempted beyond your own strength, but with the temptation will also provide the way of escape, that you may be able to endure it." He has told us that if we are living in a vital relationship with Christ, His Spirit will give us the power we need to face any situation. We need to accept this power and make it a living reality in our lives. We must remember that we are "more than conquerors" (Rom. 8:37), that we can "do all things in him who strengthens" us (Phil. 4:13). These verses are not just some high-blown rhetoric or quaint poetic expressions. They are promises of God to deal with real-life situations which we face. In fact, the trials and hardships which Paul describes in the preceding verses in both of these chapters make an unhappy marriage look pretty insignificant in comparison.

God's power to meet our needs must be kept clearly in the foreground of our thinking as it relates to marriage. In exercising His power to meet our needs, God often lets us go through suffering. But He promises that, as we accept difficulties, He will bring growth and maturity. We are not promised that by following the path of obedience we will avoid pain, but we are promised a richer life in Christ.

Charlie Brown once said that it's wonderful what proper theology will do for one's peace of mind. By contrast, it's sad to see how improper theology can mess up our lives. The incorrect idea that marriage is synonymous with the relationship puts a tremendous burden on couples. They are constantly under pressure to perform. I have known scores of couples who spend a lot of time and waste a lot of emotional energy examining their relationships to see whether or not they are going to make it. If they have a bad week or a bad couple of months, they become worried and depressed. This in itself injects still more tension into the relationship so that it becomes a vicious circle.

When couples have a proper understanding of marriage—when they are living out their permanent commitment—they are free from this constant worry. There is the security that comes from knowing that the marriage is forever, no matter what. Then when the relationship is less than ideal the partners hang in there and work at making things better, knowing that this setback cannot affect their commitment.

This is where Christian marriages have always been until the last generation or so. Our Christian parents and grandparents didn't have terrific relationships all of the time. In fact, today in many ways our marriage relationships are often much better. We have learned to communicate more freely, we know more about each other's needs, and we have the help of many good books and seminars on marriage. But though our parents may not have been blessed with ideal communication and they weren't always aware of each other's needs, they did have the one vital ingredient for success: they persevered. They understood God's design for marriage and they obeyed His commands concerning it. And God blessed them.

Perhaps our parents weren't always perfectly happy, but they were content. And after all, isn't that a prime ingredient of the Christian life? The Bible tells us to be content; it never tells us to be happy. Happiness comes to the committed Christian as a by-product of obedience. We are never promised a life which is free from pain, struggle, and disappointment. We *are* promised that, if we persevere, victory is ours.

God's word and intent regarding marriage have not suddenly changed after all these centuries. It is the culture that has changed, condoning divorce. And so the Christian community just follows along, with Christian counselors often out in front. It is time that we see where we are going and do an abrupt about-face before it is too late. The world is ever near, as a popular hymn tells us. But we don't have to—we *dare not*—take our direction from the world.

Role of Elders and Deacons

Elders and deacons can fill an important role in the lives of their pastor and his wife: encouraging them as they struggle to live the surrendered life. There are two pitfalls, however, which lay leaders should be aware of in their relationship with their pastor and his wife.

On the one hand they often put them on a pedestal so far above themselves that they can't even entertain the thought that the pastor and his wife could possibly fall into serious sin. We must all realize that even while preaching every Sunday, teaching, and praying, pastors can lose their vital relationship with Christ. While going through all the right motions and even having a certain effectiveness in teaching, counseling, etc., a minister can drift away from the Lord. And then he eventually becomes very vulnerable to Satan's attacks.

This does not happen overnight. It is a gradual thing. The pastor himself probably doesn't notice that it is happening. If he did, he would do something about it. A man doesn't have a vital relationship with Christ one day, depending on the Holy Spirit and earnestly seeking God's will for his life, and the next day hop into bed with a woman counselee. These things are usually a long time in the making. The attitude comes before the act of adultery or whatever.

If elders and deacons are spiritually sensitive, they can often detect signs of tension in the pastor's life. If you see him sagging—he's saying all the right words but his heart isn't really in it the way it once was—be a real friend to him and try to help him see what is happening.

After making the pastor aware of his spiritual low, the elder may suggest a retreat or seminar which would help him to get things back in perspective. He may have other ideas. His goal should be to help the pastor regain the surrendered life of waiting on the power of the Holy Spirit.

Another mistake which elders and deacons can make is this. Observing that the pastor has a sin problem, they simply read him the riot act. If there is already tension between the governing board and the pastor over some other matters, they probably will not be able to give him real help. They should then back off and ask the elders of a neighboring church to come in and help.

In the Presbyterian form of church government, which is my tradition, the elder is put in the role of having responsibility for the pastor's life and doctrine. This should be positive as well as negative—not just something which comes into play when the pastor gets out of line.

One way in which elders can help is by living godly, obedient lives themselves. Almost every pastor can mention certain elders who have been a help to him by their example. Older elders, especially, can be a great help to young, inexperienced pastors. My husband particularly remembers, with gratitude, the help which many of the godly elders in our first congregation gave him. One man who was exceptionally humble was an example of the totally surrendered life. Another was an inspiration in the way he always put the kingdom first in his life, in spite of great financial cost to himself and his family.

Role of Fellow Pastors

The secular society around us promotes individualism: each man takes care of his own problems. We don't interfere in anyone else's life unless we're invited. The world tells us not to poke our noses into something that isn't our business. In contrast to this, the Bible always talks in terms of fellowship, of community. We *are* our brother's keepers. First Corinthians 12 says that if one part of the body hurts, the whole body is in pain. We are responsible for each other. When we know that a person is hurting, we must find a way to get in there and help him. We must never, like the priest and the Levite, simply pass by on the other side of the road. If we do, we are just like the people on the street who ignore crimes which they witness because they don't want to get involved.

Several divorced pastors told me how disappointed they were that when their marriages were breaking up, none of their fellow pastors came forward to offer help or even just to visit. It was as if once they had gotten themselves in trouble, they'd better get themselves out of it. I talked to a couple of pastors who during college and seminary had been close friends with a pastor who later divorced. According to them they never saw their former friend anymore. One of the men commented that this pastor was "all messed up." I am sure that the one who made this comment would never deal with his own parishioner this way. If one of the members of his congregation got himself messed up, he would try to help him get straightened out. But a pastor friend who is in trouble is somehow supposed to find his own way.

Another divorced man, who is still in the parish ministry, said that his colleagues don't shun him, but they do seem to be overly interested in getting him married off again. Every time he visits with his pastor friends they are trying to fix him up with someone. They never give him any peace. In his analysis, he was a real threat to them as long as he remained single. Since his wife had left him because of pressures in the ministry, he represented what could happen to them.

We as pastors and wives need to be more sensitive to each other's needs and hurts. We should be the first ones to recognize that we have difficulties and problems as well as anyone else. And since we have no official pastor, we must learn to pastor each other. This is one area in which we can't afford to hope that someone else will fill the need.

Challenge to Clergy Couples

As pastors and wives we are in a unique position in the church. We *are* giving leadership with our marriages in one direction or another, if only by example. How a leader's personal life is conducted has tremendous consequences for good or evil. When a pastor breaks his marriage, the whole congregation suffers. Sometimes the shock waves go even farther into the Christian community. You may be able to continue your ministry (although many men find that their ministry is ruined), but you will have to live with the results of your sin.

Of course there is forgiveness. God's grace is bigger than any of our sins. But that doesn't mean that the results of sin won't continue to work themselves out. After David's sin with Bathsheba he was genuinely repentant. He realized the awful nature of his sin against God and cried out in contrition and sorrow. God forgave his sin and restored him to full fellowship. But David paid a heavy price in his family life. He was haunted for the rest of his life by unrest, rebellion, and sexual sins in his family. One of his sons raped one of his daughters, and two of his other sons each tried separately to steal the kingdom from him. The Bible lets us see some of the intense anguish that David had to bear because of his wayward family. And God tells us that this was a direct result of his sin of adultery.

Francis Shaeffer notes, "God said . . . 'thou shalt not die.' . . . God was not going to strike David down for his sin, but neither was he going to prevent it from affecting the flow of history: 'Howbeit, because by this deed thou hast given great occasion to the enemies of the Lord to blaspheme, the child also that is born unto thee shall surely die.' . . . History progresses; the things we do have their effect in history. So ripples continued from David's sin . . . on and on." [24]

The incident with Uriah's wife may have had even further ramifications. There are some biblical scholars who see this as the beginning of the downfall of the kingdom of Israel. They consider Solomon's many foreign wives and the sin of idolatry into which they led him to be a result of David's sexual sin. This in turn led to the eventual destruction of Israel.

The divorce of a pastor and his wife will inevitably have results on a congregation. For one thing, how can you counsel properly after a divorce? Your very example puts you in the position of advocating divorce. For this reason some Bible colleges and institutes will not even allow divorced people to attend, knowing that they will eventually be cast into the role of counselor.

Often the results of a pastor's divorce are more widespread and disturbing. I'm thinking of one congregation in which the pastor had had a long and fruitful ministry. After his divorce the congregation was impotent for many years before it began, slowly, to recover. Many of its members were new Christians who had identified strongly with the pastor. When he fell, they began to question everything that they had been taught. Now, many years later, the congregation has a long way to go to recover its former spiritual vitality.

But probably the most important point to keep in mind is what the church's real mission is. We are in the reconciling business—reconciling man to God, man to man, and man to himself. Our message is that God's grace and power are big enough to heal the most serious hurts a person is struggling with. How can we honestly offer this reconciling power to the world if we as pastors and wives won't avail ourselves of it? Whenever we stop short of the goal of full reconciliation, we lose the essence of the gospel and blunt the cutting edge of our ministry. We might as well go out of business if we can't live by the gospel which we preach. That is the most blatant sort of hypocrisy.

The November 17, 1978, issue of *Christianity Today* has an article about George MacDonald, a simple, poverty-stricken Scottish preacher who lived a century ago. What makes him notable is that he profoundly influenced two of this century's best Christian thinkers: G. K. Chesterton and C. S. Lewis. Chesterton says that one of MacDonald's books "made a difference to my whole existence." Lewis writes of him, "Those who receive my books kindly take . . . insufficient notice of my affiliation with George MacDonald. . . . I regarded him as my master . . . indeed, I fancy I have never written a book in which I did not quote from him."

What is so special about this man that he could call forth such praise from men of that caliber? "His life as a cleric was ill-paid and hard, made harder still when the rich deacons of his parish church censured his preaching on the mercy of God by reducing his salary." He lived a life of constant poverty, often barely avoiding literal starvation. "His resolute condemnations of anxiety come from one who has a right to speak."

The author of the article gives us the secret of MacDonald's greatness. "Obedience to God was his theme: 'We are no more to think "What should I like to do?" but "What would the Living One have me do?" ' . . . And he was deeply in love with his wife. His son commented, 'They give so realistic a picture of domestic and widely shared happiness.' "[25]

Here is a man and his wife who gave themselves to a life of surrender in the face of tremendous hardship. They weren't conformed to this world, although they were in an extremely difficult situation.

(How many of us wives would have accepted a reduction in salary to extreme poverty level without putting pressure on our husbands to fight it?) Their lives of obedience and self-denial bore fruit in their congregation, their family, and their circle of friends. Through C. S. Lewis their lives will continue to influence millions for years to come.

As we give our lives as living sacrifices, we too will influence many others. We need to look beyond the present moment of suffering and project ourselves into the future. Difficulties become easier to accept if we think not only of our personal peace but of how we are affecting the progress of the kingdom. If we give up on our marriages, there is no measuring the ill effects on future generations; if, however, we see them through, the results will be far different. God can and will use our lives of single-minded obedience to him to produce fruit far beyond what we can imagine. There may be a C. S. Lewis observing us.

If we are to be effective in our ministry, our lives must match our words. We who profess to love God and be committed to doing His work in the world must be the leaders in obedience to His commands. First John 5:3 says, "This is the love of God, that we keep his commandments. And his commandments are not burdensome."

Notes

1. "The Three Stages of Marriage" by Daniel Goldstine, Shirley Zucker-man, Hilary Goldstine and Katherine Larner, *Family Circle,* May 3, 1977.
2. *They Cry Too,* Lucille Lavender, published by Hawthorne Books, Inc., p. 97.
3. *The Living Bible,* Tyndale House Publishers.
4. "Dropouts from the Pastorate," by Ralph Heynen, *The Banner,* September 28, 1973.
5. *Form for the Ordination of Ministers of God's Word,* Publication Committee of the Christian Reformed Church.
6. *They Cry Too,* Lucille Lavender, pp. 122, 123.
7. "From Clerk to Clerk" by Louis Tamminga, *The Banner,* July 8, 1977.
8. *They Cry Too,* Lucille Lavender, p. 74.
9. Authorized King James Version.
10. Authorized King James Version.
11. Authorized King James Version.
12. Authorized King James Version.
13. *The Living Bible.*
14. *The Living Bible.*
15. Authorized King James Version.
16. Authorized King James Version.
17. *Tools for Time Management,* Edward R. Dayton, Zondervan Publishing House, p. 51.
18. "The Urgency of the Equipping Ministry" by Paul Benjamin, *Christianity Today,* September 22, 1978.
19. "The Urgency of the Equipping Ministry," by Paul Benjamin.
20. *The Greening of the Church,* Findley B. Edge, Word Books, Publisher, 1976, pp. 35-37, 39, 43.
21. *They Cry Too,* Lucille Lavender, pp. 77, 78.
22. "Divorce and Remarriage: A Fresh Biblical Perspective" by Dwight Hervey Small, *Theology, News and Notes,* March 1976.
23. *No Little People,* Francis A. Schaeffer, InterVarsity Press, pp. 128, 129.
24. *No Little People,* Francis Schaeffer, p. 129.
25. "Introducing George MacDonald" by Gary Havens, *Christianity Today,* November 17, 1978.

Bibliography

Lewis, C. S. *The Four Loves.* New York: Harcourt, Brace and Company.

Christenson, Larry. *The Christian Family.* Minneapolis, Minnesota: Bethany Fellowship.

Christenson, Larry and Nordis. *The Christian Couple.* Minneapolis, Minnesota: Bethany Fellowship.

Schaeffer, Edith. *What is a Family?* Old Tappan, New Jersey: Fleming H. Revell.

Fryling, Robert and Alice. *A Handbook for Engaged Couples.* Downers Grove, Illinois: InterVarsity Press.

Elliot, Elisabeth. *Let Me Be a Woman.* Wheaton, Illinois: Tyndale House Publishers, Inc.

McGinley, Phyllis. *Sixpence in Her Shoe.* New York: The Macmillan Company.

Dobson, James. *What Wives Wish their Husbands Knew about Women.* Wheaton, Illinois: Tyndales House Publishers, Inc.

Dobson, James. *Hide and Seek.* Old Tappan, New Jersey: Fleming H. Revell.

Commoner, Barry. *The Closing Circle.* New York: Bantam Books.

Sider, Ronald J. *Rich Christians in an Age of Hunger.* Downers Grove, Illinois: InterVarsity Press.

Engstrom, Ted, and Mackenzie, R. Alec. *Managing Your Time.* Grand Rapids, Michigan: Zondervan Publishing House.

Benjamin, Paul. *The Equipping Ministry.* Washington, D. C.: National Church Growth Research Center.

Bustanaby, Andre. "The Pastor and the Other Woman," *Christianity Today,* August 30, 1974.

Brinsmead, Robert. "Man," *Verdict,* September, 1978.

White, J. *Eros Defiled.* Downers Grove, Illinois: InterVarsity Press.

Trueblood, Elton. *The Incendiary Fellowship.* New York: Harper and Row.